AMERICA IN THE 21ST CENTURY: POLITICAL AND ECONOMIC ISSUES

FEDERAL RECOMMENDATIONS FOR IMPROVING FINANCIAL CAPABILITY

AMERICA IN THE 21ST CENTURY: POLITICAL AND ECONOMIC ISSUES

Additional books in this series can be found on Nova's website under the Series tab.

Additional e-books in this series can be found on Nova's website under the e-book tab.

AMERICA IN THE 21ST CENTURY: POLITICAL AND ECONOMIC ISSUES

FEDERAL RECOMMENDATIONS FOR IMPROVING FINANCIAL CAPABILITY

CRYSTAL M. KIRBY
EDITOR

nova publishers
New York

For permission to use material from this book please contact us:
Telephone 631-231-7269; Fax 631-231-8175
Web Site: http://www.novapublishers.com

Additional color graphics may be available in the e-book version of this book.

Library of Congress Cataloging-in-Publication Data

ISBN: 978-1-63117-038-6

Published by Nova Science Publishers, Inc. † New York

CONTENTS

PREFACE

The President's Advisory Council on Financial Capability was created January 29, 2010, by Executive Order to advise the President and the Secretary of the Treasury on ways to empower Americans to better understand and address financial matters in order to improve their financial well-being. This book includes a final report discussing the President's Advisory Council on financial capability; provides a strategic framework for employers; a resource guide on creating financially capable communities; and a guide to increasing financial capability among students, workers and residents in communities.

Chapter 1 – Report of President's Advisory Council on Financial Capability: Final Report, dated January 29, 2013.

Chapter 2 – Report of a President's Advisory Council on Financial Capability at Work: A Strategic Framework for Employers, dated September 4, 2012.

Chapter 3 – Report of President's Advisory Council on Financial Capability Communities: A Resource Guide, dated March 2012.

Chapter 4 – Paper released by the White House on Every American Financially Empowered: A Guide to Increasing Financial Capability Among Students, Workers and Residents in Communities, May 2012.

In: Federal Recommendations
Editor: Crystal M. Kirby
ISBN: 978-1-63117-038-6

Chapter 1

PRESIDENT'S ADVISORY COUNCIL ON FINANCIAL CAPABILITY: FINAL REPORT*

President's Advisory Council on Financial Capability

Americans' ability to build a secure future for themselves and their families requires the navigation of an increasingly complex financial system. As we recover from the worst economic crisis in generations, it is more important than ever to be knowledgeable about the consequences of our financial decisions. ... We recommit to improving financial literacy and ensuring all Americans have access to trustworthy financial services and products.

President Barack Obama
Presidential Proclamation –
National Financial Literacy Month
March 31, 2011

MEMBERS OF THE PRESIDENT'S ADVISORY COUNCIL ON FINANCIAL CAPABILITY

John W. Rogers (Chair), Jr., Chairman, CEO, and Chief Investment Officer, Ariel Investments

* This is an edited, reformatted and augmented version of President's Advisory Council on Financial Capability publication, dated January 29, 2013.

Amy Rosen (Vice Chair), President and CEO, Network for Teaching Entrepreneurship (NFTE)
Roland Arteaga, President and CEO, Defense Credit Union Council (DCUC)
Janie Barrera, Founding President and Chief Executive Officer of ACCION Texas Inc.
Ted Beck, President and CEO, National Endowment for Financial Education (NEFE)
Sherry Salway Black, Director, Partnership for Tribal Governance, National Congress of American Indians
John Hope Bryant, Founder, Chairman and CEO, Operation HOPE
Samuel T. Jackson, Founder, Chairman, and CEO, Economic Empowerment Initiative, Inc.
Richard Ketchum, Chairman and CEO, Financial Industry Regulatory Authority (FINRA)
Beth Kobliner, Personal Finance Commentator, Journalist, and Author
Marc Morial, President and CEO, National Urban League
Addison Barry Rand, CEO, AARP
Carrie Schwab-Pomerantz, President, Charles Schwab Foundation
Eldar Shafir, William Stewart Tod Professor of Psychology and Public Affairs, Department of Psychology and Woodrow Wilson School for Public and International Affairs, Princeton University
Kenneth Wade, Senior Community Affairs Executive, Bank of America

January 29, 2013

The Honorable Barack Obama
President of the United States
The White House
1600 Pennsylvania Avenue NW
Washington, D.C. 20500

The Honorable Neal Wolin
Acting Secretary of the Treasury
Department of the Treasury
1500 Pennsylvania Avenue NW
Washington, D.C. 20220

Dear Mr. President, Acting Secretary Wolin, and fellow citizens:

On January 29, 2010, President Barack Obama signed Executive Order 13530 creating the President's Advisory Council on Financial Capability. Our charge, to assist the American people in understanding financial matters and making informed financial decisions, remains a critical one at this particular time in our nation's history and for building a vibrant, informed citizenry.

I am pleased, on behalf of the Council, to present this final report, which provides our final recommendations. Solving the problem of financial capability is complex. Our Council hopes to help simplify the solution by highlighting just four key recommendations. Our hope is that this focus will encourage the federal government, state and local governments, tribal leaders, the private sector, and the non-profit sector to, in turn, focus their resources on ensuring real progress on this critical issue. In the interest of spurring action, for each major recommendation the Council has also used our ability, within our charter, to encourage action and begin development of tools that can be used to advance the recommendation.

The four major recommendations, along with the Council's other recommendations, share a common element: they acknowledge that financial capability is not a "stand-alone" topic to be isolated from the rest of our lives. Financial capability must be woven into the fabric of our lives—into our homes, our schools, our workplaces, our communities, even the design and regulation of the financial products and services we use.

The four major recommendations can be summarized as follows:

1) Financial education is a lifelong pursuit that needs to begin in the home with parents educating their children, continue in a child's pre-school years, continue throughout high school in preparation for post-secondary education and training, and then persist beyond. We call on experts, with the support of the federal government to encourage and support the introduction of financial literacy into homes and communities using accessible tools such as the Council's www.MoneyAsYouGrow.org, and into schools with the Council's www.MoneyAsYouLearn.org, an initiative to incorporate critical personal finance competencies into teaching of the Common Core State Standards for English and mathematics.

Many indicators, including the level of student loan debt the United States, illustrate the need and urgency of equipping our youth with the financial skills to plan for a successful future. To address this important national challenge, we encourage states and other partners to build on the www.MoneyAsYouLearn.org initiative and pursue and implement effective, evidence based strategies to integrate content within K-12 school curricula.

2) The workplace is a critical place to provide financial capability education and well-framed financial choices. Encourage the federal government and all employers to embrace an enhanced responsibility for the financial well-being of employees and share best practices in employee education and benefits, using tools such as the Council resource "Financial Capability at Work: A Strategic Framework to Guide Employers," to help employers succeed in this effort.
3) Financial capability can best be advanced in the community through the coordinated efforts of local governments, schools, post-secondary institutions, financial service providers, local business leaders and non-profits working together. Encourage the federal government to support and build upon the 110 state, local, and tribal financial capability councils to harness their resources and promote the financial well-being of their residents, especially the most economically challenged, by promoting the use of the Council's resource guide, "Creating Financially Capable Communities."
4) Financial capability can be viewed as a function of education, enlightened regulation and choice architecture. Without well-designed financial instruments, informed by an understanding of the kinds of mistakes people make, even the best-educated are likely to fail and thoughtful educational programs will be considered ineffective. Understanding what actually works will require research. Ensuring the availability of quality options and adequate protection will require appropriate regulation. Financial education researchers, behavioral economists and regulators should learn from and inform each other's work. Toward that end, the federal government should establish an online clearinghouse for research in the field of financial education and behavioral economics that is informed by rigorous research standards, like those used by the Doing What Works Clearinghouse in the Department of Education.

As we stated in our interim report, the financial crisis of 2008 shone a spotlight on the need for improved financial capability in the United States. The sub-prime lending crisis, excessive credit card and student loan debt, and the challenges facing many homeowners are often attributed to predatory practices, but they also result, in part, from both the lack of financial knowledge and inadequate access to responsibly-designed financial products and services. The Council believes that improved financial capability can help address these issues, but is even more fundamental to the challenges facing our country. A financially capable population is required for:

- restoring upward economic mobility and reducing the widening income and wealth gap;
- sparking entrepreneurship, which drives job growth; and
- having an informed civic dialogue on taxes, entitlements, government debt, and other critical issues facing our country.

The federal government should continue to spotlight, coordinate and be a leader in promoting financial capability, but it cannot do so alone. With the Council's term now concluded, we ask you to consider how the federal government can sustain and increase its focus on this important issue in a way that catalyzes the substantial efforts of the private sector, state, local, and tribal governments and the non-profit sector in addressing these issues.

We ask all those with an interest in these critical issues not only to consider these recommendations, but to use them as a springboard for action. The goal of a financially capable population is shared by all Americans, and the opportunity to help future generations make a better life than their parents is central to our values. We strongly believe that helping young Americans have the skills, knowledge and information to make smarter decisions throughout their lives will make our country stronger and more secure in the years ahead.

Sincerely,

John W. Rogers, Jr., Chair

EXECUTIVE SUMMARY

The President's Advisory Council on Financial Capability was created January 29, 2010, by Executive Order to advise the President and the Secretary of the Treasury on ways to empower Americans to better understand and address financial matters in order to improve their financial well-being.

Focus

The financial capability landscape is filled with numerous financial education choices, products and resources and yet lacks standards, measures of efficacy, and interventions with proven effectiveness. For these reasons, the Council focused on the three places financial education should be delivered to reach Americans throughout their life: school, home and community, and workplace. The Council recognized that educating people to make wise financial choices is necessary, but not wholly sufficient: an educated citizenry needs an environment with appropriate regulation and availability of quality options and tools to succeed. The Council specified as principles that its work would consolidate and boost existing efforts, leverage technology, and account for the needs of the underserved as well as the general population, while retaining a solid basis in research.

Approach

Conducting its work through four subcommittees –Youth, Underserved and Community Empowerment, Partnerships, and Research and Evaluation– the Council drew upon the expertise of its members and consulted frequently with outside experts from the financial education community, primary and secondary education community, private sector, all levels of government, and academia. Council members organized and participated in numerous listening sessions across the country and solicited input from the public to help guide its work. Subcommittees and individual Council members collaborated freely across formal lines to integrate their work. Membership of each is listed in Appendix A and Council member biographies are included in Appendix F.

Major Accomplishments

Council members benefited from more than 10 listening sessions and Council meetings on educational standards, innovative workplace financial education initiatives, behavioral economic and financial education research, and access issues for underserved populations; as well as sixty-two formally-submitted public comments on the Council's themes and principles. The Council also worked with the White House to host a Summit on Financial Capability and Empowerment. One outcome of this summit was a preliminary resource guide and toolkit entitled "Every American Financially Empowered," available at http://www.whitehouse.gov/sites/default/files/financial capability toolkit 5.10.2012.pdf.

The Council was pleased to listen, learn, and encourage the following actions:

Sparked Treasury's MyMoney App Up Challenge, an innovative contest to encourage development of ideas for mobile apps that promote financial capability and financial access.

Conceived www.MoneyAsYouGrow.org, an online tool that gives families a way to teach kids, from ages three to 23 and beyond, the essential money lessons they need to know as they grow. The website has received more than 500,000 visits since its launch at the White House Summit on Financial Capability and Empowerment.

Encouraged the United States' participation in the financial literacy modules of the 2012 and 2015 Programme for International Student Assessment (PISA).

Catalyzed the development of Money as You Learn (forthcoming at www.MoneyAsYouLearn.org), which provides concrete tools for educators showing how personal finance can provide appropriate context and content for mathematics and English language arts teaching.

Celebrated the nine inaugural winners of a newly created private-sector award program: Workplace Leaders in Financial Education (WLIFE), which recognizes employers that provide outstanding financial education to their employees.

Created and disseminated "Financial Capability at Work: A Strategic Framework to Guide Employers," (http://www.treasury.gov/resource-center/financialeducation/Documents/PACFC%20Financial%20Capability%20at%20Work.pdf) a resource guide for employers to help them provide quality financial capability opportunities in the workplace, including best practices, resources and supporting research.

Encouraged the formation of over 110 local financial capability councils and created a toolkit (http://www.treasury.gov/resource-center/financial-education/Documents/Local%20Guide%20%20Creating%20Financially%20Capable%20Communities.pdf) to help community leaders create these councils and take immediate positive actions in their communities.

Compiled financial education and behavioral finance research studies and identified key knowledge gaps and national research priorities to the federal government's Financial Literacy and Education Commission.

Recommendations

Through its life, the full Council reviewed, discussed and unanimously approved 15 recommendations to the President and the Secretary of the Treasury. A brief summary of each of the recommendations is found in Appendix B (and more detailed explanations of each are elsewhere in this report), but we have highlighted four recommendations that stand above the rest. The recommendations share a common element: they acknowledge that financial capability is not a "stand-alone" topic to be isolated from the rest of our lives. Financial capability must be woven into the fabric of our lives—into our homes, our schools, our workplaces, our communities, even the design and regulation of the products we use.

The Council's four major recommendations include a focus on:

- **YOUTH:** Integrate important aspects of personal finance into teaching of math and English language arts Common Core State Standards for K-12 education as well as other subjects.
  Status: The Money as You Learn initiative is underway through collaboration among developers and leaders of the Common Core State Standards, Jump$tart Coalition for Personal Financial Literacy, Council for Economic Education, teachers and other experts. A website, MoneyAsYouLearn.org, is currently in development.
  This approach has already been endorsed not only by the Council but also by leaders in the education and financial education communities including: Achieve, American Federation of Teachers, Council for Economic Education, Jump$tart Coalition for Personal Financial Literacy, National Education Association, National Endowment for Financial Education; National Urban League, Mitchell Chester (Massachusetts Commissioner of Education and Governing Board Chair of Partnership for Assessment of Readiness for College and Careers), Steven Grossman (Massachusetts Treasurer and Receiver General), and Cami Anderson (Superintendent Newark, NJ Public Schools).
  The Financial Literacy and Education Commission, led by the Department of the Treasury, is considering how best to support this effort given resources available, and agency missions and authorities.
- **COMMUNITIES AND FAMILIES:** That the President and the Secretary of the Treasury encourage the creation of councils at the

state, local and tribal level to help improve the financial capability of citizens.

Status: An estimated 110 councils are being formed, according to the National Conference of Black Mayors, with more possible. The "Creating Financially Capable Communities" resource guide was developed to help localized efforts and is available at http://www.treasury.gov/resource-center/financial-education/Documents/Local%20Guide%20-%20Creating%20Financially%20Capable%20Communities.pdf. The Department of Treasury is reviewing and considering other ways to support implementation of this recommendation, given resources, mission and authorities.

- **WORKPLACE:** That the federal government encourage employers to improve the financial capability of their employees and support that effort by promoting and disseminating "Financial Capability at Work," a resource guide for employers that includes a framework of best practices, resources and supporting research to help employers create and enhance successful workplace financial capability programs.

  Status: The resource "Financial Capability at Work" is publicly available at http://www.treasury.gov/resource-center/financial-education/Documents/PACFC%20Financial%20Capability%20at%20Work.pdf. The Department of the Treasury is working with Department of Labor, Small Business Administration, and others to develop approaches to implement key aspects of the recommendation and that ensure necessary consumer protection in place to assure a healthy delivery system for financial decision assistance, consistent with their statutory missions and authorities, as well as their resource priorities.

- **RESEARCH & EVALUATION:** That the Department of the Treasury, in collaboration with the Financial Literacy and Education Commission, explore the possibility of building and sustaining a collaboration hub for research in the field of financial education and behavioral economics that is informed by the rigorous research standards used by the Doing What Works Clearinghouse in the Department of Education, subject to resources available to support such a website.

  Status: The Department of Treasury will consult with the Department of Education and other agencies to assess this recommendation consistent with their statutory missions and authorities as well as their resource priorities.

Financial Capability Challenges and Opportunities in the United States

Although there is general consensus that Americans should have the opportunity to learn and exercise sound personal finance practices, there are numerous indicators that many of us are not financially capable.

In one recent study, adults scored a grade of C in financial literacy, while high school students mainly received failing grades.[1] Add to this the real financial constraints imposed by a difficult economy and the results can be devastating. For example, another study cites that 49 percent of Americans indicated that it was somewhat or very difficult for them to cover their expenses and pay their bills in a typical month. Roughly half (51 percent) said they sometimes carried over a balance on their credit card(s) and were charged interest. And 12 percent reported that their spending in the past year exceeded their income. Additionally, the majority of Americans do not have a "rainy-day" fund for unanticipated financial emergencies and are not adequately preparing for their children's college education and their own retirement.[2]

While financial education cannot fix financial misfortune stemming from unemployment or high medical expenses, it can give Americans the resources, tools and encouragement to manage their money with greater confidence and help more Americans reach their financial goals.

Toward a Better Understanding

Many researchers now believe that financial capability has several critical components: at least a minimal understanding of financial issues needed to be able to function in an increasingly complex and demanding world; and a market context that allows for an average consumer – not to mention a less-advantaged person – to successfully navigate the many complexities given her newly acquired knowledge. For example, if you train people extremely well on financial matters, and then place them in an environment where the right products are nearly impossible to find, or where they need to sign a 60-page document in "legalese," with seemingly incomprehensible clauses, and without trusted advisors, their knowledge, no matter how sophisticated, is bound to fail.

Financial education, both formal and informal, is just one component of financial capability. Two additional areas of importance contribute to the nuanced interaction between human proclivities and the arena of financial decision making. This suggests that we recognize that financial capability is balanced upon three legs:

1) Financial education (formal and informal) that delivers the basic understanding;
2) Regulation and consumer protection that assure some minimal ability to rely on available products and services; and
3) Thoughtful design of options – what behavioral economics has come to call "choice architecture" – in a way that facilitates the successful application of what has been learned.

The three legs play a critical role in promoting financial capability—they each are strongest when used together and in isolation are more likely to fail. Financial capability relies on three key pillars that support informed and smart financial decision-making. Without consumer understanding, healthy market competition is unlikely to yield increased well-being, since consumers will simply fail to avail themselves of the choices that are best for them. On the other hand, in the absence of meaningful regulation and consumer protection, even the best-educated consumers will fail. And with good options available in the market, even informed consumers will fare better with sound regulatory protections in place.

Opportunities

Recent research has contributed much to our basic understanding of the potential for greater financial capability among American consumers. Now we have the opportunity to build upon this foundation with rigorous exploration of the components that are essential for success.

Financial education, if encouraged and made widely available, is the intervention most familiar to the average consumer. In fact, we are able to get numerous financial lessons through many different channels, and should look for evidence that those lessons are helpful. Beginning with teachable moments in the home, every parent, directly or by omission, is a financial educator to their children, and every child is a learner. Young people continuously absorb financial intelligence and put it into practice as soon as they decide how to spend their first coins. Those who eventually enter the financial system encounter increasingly complex financial instruments throughout their lives.

As adults, we make increasingly complex decisions about what to do with our money, and appreciate familiarity with personal finance concepts through formal and informal financial education. Workplaces also provide numerous opportunities, particularly around "life events," such as adding family members, or retirement, for financial education provided by a trusted source, the employer, at key decision-making moments.

Challenges

Although it seems simple, then, to prescribe financial education as the primary means to achieve financial capability, the challenges are much more complex. During its term, the Council has consulted with experts and researchers to learn more about the barriers to financial capability.

Common Human Behaviors

Driven by biology and our psychological biases, human beings inherently face challenges in navigating a complex financial world mired by misinformation, bureaucratic processes, and short-term costs associated with discounted long-term gains. On average, human beings are prone to procrastination—putting off difficult decisions that cost time and money to deal with today, but if taken have the potential to reap major gains later in life.

In 2010, an extensive review of financial behavior research consolidated seminal findings from the past 30 years to explain many of the factors that hold people back when it comes to their finances.[3] This literature review found that:

People tend to favor short-term action and rewards sooner rather than later, and find it difficult to connect to their needs far into the future. The preference for a small reward now versus a large reward later ("delay discounting"), the ability to postpone or forego pleasures now for a future reward ("future orientation"), the inability to delay gratification, and self-control all impact decisions that weigh the present against the future.

Risk aversion and having more sensitivity to losses than gains ("negativity bias") impact the ability to commit to financial action, particularly, it appears, among women.

Overall confidence in one's self and confidence in one's ability to succeed at tasks (self-efficacy) have profound effects on financial decision making. Overconfidence can lead to riskier financial behaviors, such as investing in products that are not fully understood and reacting to economic news and market swings. Under-confidence can lead to excessive timidity (such as long-term "investing" in cash resulting in erosion through inflation) or dependence on advice that may leave the consumer financially vulnerable.

The ability to make dispassionate and objective financial decisions is affected by the tendency to use a specific value for an asset, such as the acquisition price ("framing" or "anchoring"), following the crowd (unconscious "herding"), and relying on information that confirms one's beliefs ("attribution bias"). Consequently, for example, people don't like to sell a stock or price a home for sale at a lower value than what they paid for it.

Procrastination, "choice overload" (an overwhelming number of and/or confusing choices lead to an inability to make any choice at all), and the propensity to plan affect when and how a person initiates financial plans and actions. Whereas starting to save earlier for retirement can result in greater outcomes, procrastination can cause detrimental shortfalls.

"Moral hazard" (taking more risk when resulting losses will be covered by somebody else) creates a climate in which individuals may do less research on financial products, or stretch themselves to take on excessive debt, because options such as bankruptcy are available to discharge their liabilities.

External Impacts

Not all shortcomings in the arena of financial capability can be attributed to psychology and personality. In 2010, researchers and experts examined many external factors and developments which impact Americans and their financial lives.[4]

"What creates the [financial literacy] crisis is not a sudden decline in financial knowledge, but the rapid expansion of what consumers need to know," the researchers stated. Consumers now need greater sophistication when choosing financial products due to the financial deregulation that started in the U.S. in the 1970s and 1980s, and the financial innovations of the past 30 years, such as adjustable rate loans, teaser rate loans, and low documentation loans. Debt securitized by these "imperfectly understood" offerings arose on the investment side as well.

During this time period, consumers have been forced to assume greater responsibility for retirement planning and risk assessment in both accumulation and decumulation (spending down) of assets. Social Security benefits replace a smaller portion of pre-retirement earnings than ever before, and the dramatic shift from defined benefit to defined contribution plans requires a higher level of management by individuals and their families.

Economic and technological trends have disrupted old rules of thumb, illustrating the need to keep financial awareness and knowledge up to date. For example, old advice about lowering income tax withholding in order to take advantage of the ability to save may be less useful to many taxpayers in a low-interest rate period. Similarly, the financial lessons someone may have learned in high school 20 years ago, may no longer be salient with today's financial products and services.

Barriers to Financial Education

Although the obstacles to financial capability are complex and daunting, Americans still need and benefit from financial education. However, this approach is beset with several possible barriers:

Clutter: The number of financial education resources to choose from is overwhelmingly large. At the same time, quality and efficacy indicators are sorely lacking and there is no clear relationship between the quality of a program and its availability. As a result, those who want to pick from the available pool may suffer choice overload. Research shows that when there are large numbers of choices people are less likely to make a choice.[6]

Lack of standards: There are no universal standards to evaluate the quality and effectiveness of financial education programs and resources. Evaluation practices are dependent on funding, time, human resources, and evaluation design and expertise. The inconsistency, inadequacy and mismatching of standards leads to incongruous results that cannot be used to rate programs.[7]

Persistent financial exclusion: Low- and moderate-income families, minority households, and certain persistently under-resourced communities are likely lacking resources, knowledge, experience and access for themselves and to share with the next generation. The challenges in such communities are great and multifaceted, and solutions must address complex needs. Additionally, many populations lack access to safe and affordable products to meet their needs. Approximately one-fourth (25.6 percent) of U.S. households are considered unbanked or underbanked,[8] These Americans may face more decisions about financial products and services that financial education and information would help address, in order to make choices that can help meet their financial needs and goals.

Reluctant venues (schools): Many primary and secondary schools may shy away from offering financial education classes due to lack of qualified teachers and lack of time and space in mandatory curricula. Only nine states have formal requirements to assess students' financial literacy.[9] Less than 20 percent of primary and secondary teachers believe they are adequately prepared to teach personal finance topics.[10]

Reluctant venues (workplace): Many employers fear liability issues if they provide financial education to their workforce and shelter themselves behind retirement-centric presentations by their 401(k) providers. Those willing to offer comprehensive financial education often are discouraged by material and human resource constraints.

Limited research: Impactful pedagogy is based on content- and audience-specific research, both of which are sparse in the emerging field of behavioral economics and financial education. Although the body of knowledge is growing, many significant gaps exist. Scant funding is available for researchers in this arena, especially for longitudinal research, slowing progress in developing research-based solutions.

Success in Financial Education

To successfully bring financial education to all who could benefit from it requires bold – but common sense – action to overcome these challenges. Attaining financial capability at any age is a continuous process comprising knowledge, behavior change, demonstration and action, standards and learning objectives.

Fortunately, we can build solutions based on what we have learned works, which means acknowledging learning and behavior change requires:

NOT JUST ONE, BUT MANY LESSONS: Financial education sticks better and is more likely to lead to action the more frequently one hears it, sees it, reads it.[11] Parents can start teaching children as young as 2 about money, and there is no age cutoff – financial education continues to be needed and relevant throughout all life stages.

CONNECTING LEARNING WITH DOING: Financial education is more effective when delivered as close in time to a financial decision as possible – the decision equivalent of "point of purchase" -although financial educators advocate for access to financial information even further upstream. For example, when one seeks to buy a home, financial education at the time of initial consideration can help the consumer wisely choose the home's features (number of bedrooms, bathrooms, lot size, granite countertops, etc.) based on affordability, as opposed to selecting a specific house and then figuring out whether or not he can afford it.

CONVENIENT & ACCESSIBLE OPPORTUNITIES FOR ACTION: Financial education in the workplace makes sense – it is where people make their money and their decisions about financial benefits such as health care coverage and retirement savings. Employers who offer financial education may be able to mitigate increased health care costs, absences and lower productivity brought on by financial stress and worry.[12]

ENGAGING MATERIAL AND APPROACHES: Although adults can learn in classroom settings, financial education is better absorbed when it is delivered via different techniques to appeal to the many different learning styles of adults. Research shows greater success when instructors use learner experiences and engage learners in group discussions, and use stories built around diverse characters or drawn from educators' own lives.[13] Similarly, lessons for children should be enlivened with relevant topics, role playing, games, experiential learning techniques, peer discussion and technology-based information delivery to make the greatest impact.

COMMON-SENSE TIMING: The impact of a financial education lesson is magnified when it can be tied to an immediate decision (helping a child comparison shop with his allowance money) or a current situation (being affected by the national recession). For teens, work experience is a compelling teachable moment, tied with school-based financial education as the second greatest influence (after parents) on good financial attitudes and behaviors.[14]

USE SCHOOLS SMARTLY: Financial education in schools has been shown by research to be the second most important influencer of good financial management practices in young people, after parents.[15] Well-designed and well-funded state mandates, course requirements and testing requirements that weave financial education into standard curricula would insure that most children receive it at least once in grades kindergarten through 12. Critically, research shows that better-prepared teachers will make a positive difference in school-based delivery of financial education. Teachers are more likely to teach financial education if they are confident in their abilities to do so, and well-prepared teachers experience significant increases in their knowledge and behavior and are much more likely to teach the content.[16, 17]

FAMILY ENGAGEMENT IS CRITICAL: Research indicates that the number one influence on young people's financial behavior is their parents,[18] and that communities also play a vital role in helping to shape families' financial decisions. Parents and other adults influence children's behavior by serving as good role models, setting clear and positive expectations, and talking directly to kids about money. But many adults feel ill-equipped to teach kids and overwhelmed by the information around them.[19,20] They need resources and tools that use down-to-earth language and provide sound, clear principles to help them be the best role models and teachers they can be.

TECHNOLOGY INNOVATIONS: Technology-based tools hold promise to help Americans make more informed financial decisions and to address some of the barriers to financial education, including making it faster and more convenient to access information, obtain more in-depth advice and guidance, and to share financial goals among one's social networks. [21] In particular, the wide penetration of mobile phones presents a scalable way to deliver real-time, actionable financial information; helping families make wiser financial decisions in the immediate term and helping them achieve longer-term financial goals. [22]

Beyond Financial Education

Again we note that financial education, both formal and informal, is just one component of financial capability. Two additional areas of importance contribute to the nuanced interaction between human proclivities and the arena of financial decision making.

Regulatory and consumer protection oversight is needed to guarantee a minimal adherence to fair rules. Additionally, a decision context structured to allow for the flourishing of human capability also is important. Without adequately designed contexts and minimal protections, even the effectively educated might be observed to fail. In such contexts as these, effective educational programs may be unduly dismissed. Conversely, in well-designed decision contexts, where the "right" choices are easier to come by, even less thorough educational attainments may thrive.

A person well educated about consumer lending options, for example, may prefer a home equity loan to pay off debt, but have only less-appealing vehicles, such as a credit card or payday loan, available to him. When education and the right contextual environment coexist, however, consumers can achieve remarkably more successful results, despite their human proclivities. The weaknesses in building financial capability can – and needs to – be overcome. And that can be achieved by providing effective education in a product and decision context designed to help consumers choose the best financial options according to their goals and values.

This view of financial capability should be disseminated among researchers, practitioners and policy makers. A shared understanding of some of the main features underlying financial capability may lead to more successful implementation of research and evaluation, education, consumer protection, choice architecture and product defaults, and, eventually, to significant advances where they might matter to American citizens, especially those of lower income, the most.

There is extensive opportunity for government, particularly the federal government, to contribute to the advancement of regulatory and consumer protection oversight, as well as to the thoughtful design of options within a healthy financial decision context. Each financial "touchpoint" that the federal government has with citizens presents an opportunity to consider how all three elements necessary for success are incorporated into the delivery mechanism of the financial assistance or product. Is adequate education included? Are the necessary consumer protections in place? And is the choice architecture appropriately structured?

Themes and Principles

The Council's assessment of these challenges and opportunities led us to adopt a set of principles which guided our recommendations, as well as a set of themes to focus our efforts. The themes and principles were published for public comment in the Federal Register.[23]

Principles

The Council believes that its recommendations must embody several principles if they are to succeed in affecting financial behaviors. Specifically, our recommendations should:

Be focused, impactful, executable and have measureable outcomes. The Secretary and President deserve recommendations that can be practically, and quickly, implemented and judged for their effectiveness in changing behavior.

Align with, consolidate and boost, rather than supplant, existing efforts of the private, for-profit, non-profit, and governmental sectors. There are countless extraordinary financial capability efforts underway, many of which simply need help achieving better awareness and broader distribution.

Be consistent with the latest findings in financial education and behavioral economics. Literacy for its own sake is not the goal; financial capability means knowledge-based *action*.

Address issues related to the entire population, and where appropriate, take into account the particular needs of traditionally underserved populations (e.g., women, minorities, low and moderate income consumers, and the elderly). Recommendations should account for the different needs of different segments of our population.

Leverage the use of technology to engage, inform, and impact behavior. Technology can help us provide content and coaching closely associated with "teachable moments" in financial capability, as well as scalable, personalized information and advice.

Sixty-two comments were received from individuals, nonprofit organizations, financial institutions, government, associations and academia. The principles were received with great enthusiasm and the majority of the commenters declared them "right on target". Some of the points highlighted by the commenters include: the need for more research to determine effective approaches that deliver positive outcomes; and the need to raise public awareness of the need for financial. In addition, integration was emphasized many times, for example, integrating financial education into existing adult programs such as social services or other government touch points, integrating financial education into existing K-12 curricula. The positive role that technology can play, and how to provide teachers with the appropriate training were also common areas of comment.

Themes

Based on a review of the research, the Council decided to concentrate its final recommendations into three "venues" where our citizens are likely to be receptive to effective financial capability education and improved access. (In all three cases, we considered the particular needs of traditionally underserved populations). These three venues, or themes, are:

Theme I. Financial education should take its rightful place in American schools.

Rationale: Financial illiteracy is widespread in the United States and Americans, including students, are worse off because of this. Low levels of financial literacy appear to be tied to higher rates of being "unbanked," higher levels of indebtedness, lower rates of wealth accumulation, and lower rates of retirement planning.[24] Eighty-two percent of Americans[25] and eighty-nine percent of teachers[26] think personal finance should be taught to all students at least as early as high school. In particular, navigating whether and how to pursue higher education and how to finance this investment is critical, but many students appear unprepared to do it. Two million enrolled college students eligible for Pell Grants did not apply for federal aid, leaving money on the table;[27] two-thirds of students taking private loans did not exhaust more affordable, flexible federal aid first;[28] and at a time when student loan debt now exceeds credit card debt in America, student loan defaults are on the rise.

Students need to be provided with effective financial education *before* they enter into financial contracts, yet:

Financial education and debt management programs aimed at students receiving federal student loans are unevenly administered and rarely evaluated.

While there are many financial literacy programs aimed at America's students from pre-kindergarten through college and beyond, there is a dearth of research on the effectiveness of these programs and their impact on subsequent behavior.

Theme II. We should build a financially capable workforce and retiree community, which is necessary for a stable and globally competitive economy.

Rationale: Delivering financial education and access in the workplace – and providing employers with cost-effective models of high-quality financial guidance and related benefits – has the potential to positively impact 134 million Americans.[29] Encouraging workplace financial education and access can drive positive behavioral change during the life stages at which most adults make critical decisions regarding savings, retirement planning, insurance and other benefits.

What American adults actually know about personal finance and math is sharply lower than what they think they know. Almost half (48 percent) who gave themselves the highest score in math were not able to do two calculations involving interest rates and inflation.[30]

Seventy-six percent of Americans say they are stressed about money.[31]

Over two-thirds of employers say that financial stress contributes to health costs at their company. Fifty-eight percent say that financial "illness" contributes to employee absences at their companies, and 78 percent also agree that employees are less productive at work when worrying about personal financial problems.[32]

Employee Assistance Program providers have seen an 88 percent increase in requests for help with financial matters since the economic downturn began.[33]

Theme III. Americans should also learn the core concepts of personal finance at the heart of their lives— in their families and in their communities.

Rationale: Families and the communities in which they live are the core social and economic units of American society -- the key environments within which financial capability can be taught and learned with long-lasting effectiveness. Responsibility for modeling and teaching financial capability begins in the family and extends to the local community of businesses, financial institutions, schools, non-profits, and even places of worship. Parents need to start the conversation (e.g., "talk to your kids about money"), and we need to provide the public, especially low and moderate income families, the learning tools and the financial access to become financially capable.

Even if parents do not model positive financial behaviors in front of their children, they influence positive financial behaviors through their expectations for their children. Also, they influence their children through direct teaching.[34]

In addition, a growing body of research has been coalescing around the notion that young children can grasp rudimentary financial concepts.[35]

Among youth who expected to graduate from a four-year college, those with a savings account in their name were approximately six times more likely to attend college than those with no account.[36]

"Communities are an important entry point for social change...." They affect individual and family wellbeing and their influences are amenable to change.[37]

The financial crisis of 2008, in part, demonstrated the lack of understanding of basic financial management information and skills, and the lack of access to fair, affordable, and appropriate financial products and services, which was costly to society and disproportionately impacted America's low- and middle-income earners. Our country loses valuable human capital as Americans, who struggle for daily financial survival, are unable to pursue higher education or focus their talents on innovation, entrepreneurship and intellectual contributions to the nation's progress.

With respect to the themes, the public comments were very supportive as well. A significant number of commenters agree that theme one is very important and they thought financial education in schools should be mandatory. Many also agreed that schools and teachers are not provided adequate resources to fulfill the theme's goals. Most commenters believe that schools must be provided with more funding and teachers must receive training in order to fulfill the goal of this theme. Regarding theme two, many commenters agreed that an effective way to provide financial capability to adults is by encouraging employers to incorporate financial capability in the work environment. A few commenters recommended that employers should be given incentives to start financial education initiatives such as tax credits or company recognition. Lastly, theme three had numerous commenters express support because they believed that financial capability activities in families and communities will help create a long-lasting effect. Commenters also emphasized that interpersonal interactions to communicate about finances can be very effective.

The public comments were helpful in confirming that the Council was on the right track, was generally very supportive of the principles and themes, did not suggest that the principles or themes should be altered, and were used to further focus our final recommendations.

Recommendations and Accomplishments Youth Subcommittee

Purpose

The Youth Subcommittee focused on recommendations to improve the financial capability of our nation's young people to better prepare future generations to understand the complex everyday financial decisions that they face. Research reveals that parents are the single biggest influence on a child's financial capability. Moreover, with young Americans facing a record $1 trillion in student loan debt, the Youth Subcommittee recognizes that financial literacy is essential to boosting college completion rates and sending young people into the workforce with a manageable debt load. As a result, our efforts have targeted the role that homes and families, as well as schools and communities, can play in engaging our nation's youth.

Accomplishments

Money as You Learn. The Council has set a path towards exposing more students to essential personal finance skills by integrating personal finance knowledge into classes where our young people are learning to read, write and do math. This approach is timely. Forty-five states and the District of Columbia recently banded together to adopt the Common Core State Standards in K-12 mathematics and English Language Arts designed to prepare students for success in college and careers. As a result, educators are working hard to ensure that teaching and learning reflect these new standards for academic knowledge and skills and provide students the opportunity to apply their knowledge in real world contexts. While personal finance classes will remain (and hopefully grow) as elective offerings, by connecting personal finance to what students are learning in their core classes, we can strengthen both the teaching of personal finance and the teaching of the Common Core State Standards.

The Council has identified key next steps on the path towards this goal. These include: immediately mapping how essential personal finance knowledge and skills can be integrated into teaching of the Common Core State Standards and, over time, coalescing around one set of personal finance standards for the field; developing a robust, web-based set of high quality and easily accessible tools and materials, including mathematical tasks and identification of non-fiction texts and close reading exemplars; aligning existing personal finance programs with the demands of the Common Core State Standards; and investing in research and evaluation on the teaching of financial literacy. Collaboration among Council members, developers and leaders of the Common Core State Standards, financial education experts and teachers has already led to an initial mapping showing where essential personal finance concepts and skills can appropriately be integrated into teaching of the standards as well as to the development of mathematical tasks and identification of non-fiction texts. A new website, www.MoneyAs YouLearn.org, will offer guidance to teachers and school districts by offering lesson plans, problem sets, nonfiction texts and other resources that elucidate the topic of personal finance within the context of the Common Core.

This *Money as You Learn* approach has already been endorsed not only by the Council but also by leaders in the education and financial education communities including: Achieve, American Federation of Teachers, Council for Economic Education, Jump$tart Coalition for Personal Financial Literacy, National Education Association; National Endowment for Financial Education, National Urban League; Mitchell Chester (Massachusetts Commissioner of Education and Governing Board Chair, Partnership for Assessment of Readiness for College and Careers), Steven Grossman (Massachusetts Treasurer and Receiver General), and Cami Anderson (Superintendent Newark Public Schools)

The Council recommends that the President champion this *Money as You Learn* approach and instruct the Financial Literacy and Education Commission, and its member agencies, to take all possible steps to advance it. The Council also calls on national financial literacy organizations and their state and local partners to embrace *Money as You Learn* and to build an enduring initiative that will improve the financial capability of our young people for years to come.

Money As You Learn Materials Are Included As Appendix C

Money as You Grow. In early 2011, the Council's Youth Subcommittee began a 16-month effort to distill the dozens of existing guidelines, standards, and research into one document with age-appropriate concepts written in clear, accessible language. The result is MoneyAsYouGrow.org, an online, interactive tool for families that presents 20 milestones kids need to know as they grow, along with behavior-changing activities designed with the best research and information available. At its April 9, 2012, meeting the Council unanimously approved a recommendation that the President encourage federal agencies to promote and utilize *Money as You Grow* as one tool to improve the financial capability of America's youth. The initiative was launched at the May 10, 2012, White House Summit on Financial Capability and Empowerment.

MoneyAsYouGrow.org has had no advertising budget, and yet as of December 30, 2012, a total of 524,897 individuals had visited the site, driven primarily through word of mouth on social media websites. More than half of all visitors arrive at MoneyAsYouGrow.org via Pinterest.com, a site popular among women, especially mothers. More than 100 media outlets have reported on MoneyAsYouGrow.org, including *Time*, *U.S. News and World Report*, and the *Washington Post.* The initiative earned the praise of National Economic Council Director Gene Sperling, Domestic Policy Council Director Cecilia Munoz, and Secretary of Education Arne Duncan. Thousands of *Money as You Grow* posters have been distributed to or downloaded by the general public.

The breadth and depth of response to *Money as You Grow* has been overwhelming—from a Volunteer Income Tax Assistance (VITA) site in Minnesota; to the Fort McCoy Army Community Service network in Wisconsin; to a group of elementary schools in the Sharon, Pennsylvania, school district; to an education program in Poland that wants to adapt the materials for use there. Nearly two dozen partners, with a collective reach in excess of 50 million members, have signed on to promote *Money as You Grow*, including the Federal Reserve Bank of Chicago, the American Library Association, the National Association of Elementary School Principals, the National PTA, and Junior Achievement. In September, the American Library Association's Association for Library Service to Children selected MoneyAsYouGrow.org as one of its Great Websites for Kids.

Money As You Grow materials can be found online at http://www.treasury.gov/resource-center/financialeducation/Documents/Money%20as%20You%20Grow.pdf

PISA Financial Capability Module Implemented. In 2011 the Council approved the Youth Subcommittee's recommendation that the United States participate in the financial literacy test given by the 2012 Programme for International Student Assessment (PISA). In 2012, the Department of Education, at the Council's urging, took the lead and agreed to fund this important assessment. The results of the first ever PISA examination of high school students' financial literacy will be released in 2014, and we anticipate the findings will give us a clear understanding of young Americans' financial knowledge, both as a cohort and in comparison to 15-year-olds from other countries.

Summaries of the full recommendations are found in Appendix B.

Recommendations and Accomplishments Partnerships Subcommittee

Purpose

The Partnerships Subcommittee was charged with strengthening and enhancing coordination between public and private-sector financial capability resources to better equip consumers with critical financial skills. Subcommittee members have focused on two overarching goals:

Supporting leadership, coordination and role clarity among federal, tribal, state and local agencies on the issues of financial education, access and empowerment. More than 20 federal agencies provide financial education and/or support for such programs, and while the Financial Literacy and Education Commission has in recent years made significant progress in addressing overlap and promoting the sharing of best practices, more can be done. At the same time, an ever-increasing number of tribal, state and local governments seem to be recognizing the importance of financial capability in their communities. The subcommittee believes that the development of cross-sector groups to coordinate on both the strategy for and the delivery of financial education has the potential to be an enormously important component of a successful long-term effort at improving the financial capability of communities.

Encouraging employers in the government, private and non-profit sectors to become a primary delivery point for financial education. Such an effort has the potential to reach more than 134 million working Americans[38] at a time when financial matters are extremely relevant. Employers tend to be trusted deliverers of key financial skills, and have an increasing incentive to ensure employees are free of financial stress at the workplace. But there has been, to date, little coordinated effort to provide financial capability materials and resources to employers that want to embrace this role. The Subcommittee seized on the opportunity to for the federal government to lead by example, the development of a more robust employer-centered financial capability effort.

Accomplishments

Workplace Financial Education Initiative. A central focus of the Subcommittee has been improving the financial capability of the American workforce by using the employer as a delivery mechanism for financial capability resources to employees. To help employers in this goal, the Subcommittee developed a guide, "Financial Capability at Work: A Strategic Framework to Guide Employers." This document encourages employers to become leaders and role models by voluntarily providing information and programs to employees in five fundamental areas, and working toward advanced features. The guide includes details on the five fundamentals, examples of the types of advanced features that companies should aspire to, and numerous vetted resources, programs and information that employers can use to educate employees.

The information gathered is the result of collaboration with and input from more than 75 companies, trade and professional associations, and nonprofit organizations that provided valuable perspective about how best to set achievable goals and produce landscape-changing results. The Council approved a recommendation to designate the Department of Labor and the Small Business Administration as the federal government's lead agencies in the effort to expand workplace financial education and to dedicate staff and resources to the promotion and dissemination of the guide. Of course, any initiative these agencies undertake in this area must be consistent with their statutory mission and authority as well as their resource priorities. In addition, to address concerns expressed by some companies in their comments, the recommendation encourages the President to direct the Department of Labor as part of its current retirement plan participant protection regulatory projects to review a 1996 Interpretive Bulletin on investment education for employees responsible for directing investments in their 401(k) and similar retirement accounts, with the objective of contributing to the advancement of financial decision assistance with necessary consumer protections in place to ensure healthy delivery mechanisms.

Federal Government Workplace Financial Education Initiative. The Subcommittee believes that the federal government should be modeling best practices for the private and non-profit sectors by providing outstanding financial capability resources to the approximately 2 million federal employees. The Council concurred with a Subcommittee recommendation calling on the President to direct federal agencies to improve the financial capability of their employees. After consulting with the Office of Personnel Management (OPM), the Subcommittee encouraged such elements of this approach include the creation of a centralized repository of financial capability resources at OPM and use of such resources by federal agency human resources leaders to enhance the financial capability of each agency's employees. OPM plans to develop the database, including a speakers' bureau of experts from around the federal government who are willing to speak at employee education events at other agencies. The database will be included on a new financial capability resources web page on the OPM's HR University web site and is expected to be operational in early 2013.

State and Local Councils Initiative. A recommendation was approved by the Council to call upon the President and the Secretary of the Treasury encourage the creation of Financial Capability Councils, modeled on the President's Advisory Council, at the state, local and tribal level. The Subcommittee believes strongly that these local councils can help communities pull together to address the specific financial capability needs and challenges particular to their community. Working closely with the Underserved and Community Empowerment Subcommittee, the Partnerships Subcommittee developed a guide on how to launch a local Financial Capability Council, which also included a set of "best practices" – steps that can be taken quickly and easily by a local council to have an immediate impact in the community. The guide answers such questions as who should be on a council and what steps they should take to create change in their community. The guide can be found on the Treasury website at http://www.treasury.gov/resource-center/financial-education/Documents/Local%20Guide%20%20Creating%20Financially%20Capable%20Communities.pdf.

Workplace Leaders in Financial Education Award. The Council approved a recommendation by the Partnerships Subcommittee recommending that the Treasury Department support the Workplace Leaders in Financial Education Award, administered by the American Institute of Certified Public Accountants (AICPA) and the Society for Human Resources Management (SHRM). This award was launched in 2011, based upon a recommendation of the President's Council on Financial Literacy in 2008. More than 300 applications were received and nine organizations were named winners by the panel of judges. Winners were recognized during the January 2012 meeting of the President's Advisory Council on Financial Capability. The application period for the 2013 awards open in December 2012, and winners will be announced later in 2013.

Summaries of the full recommendations are found in Appendix B.

Recommendations and Accomplishments
Underserved and Community Empowerment Subcommittee

Purpose

Those who felt the recent economic recession the hardest were those from underserved communities, made vulnerable by a lack financial education and stability. The Subcommittee on the Underserved and Community Empowerment focused on improving the financial capability of individuals from low to moderate income environments. The ideas advanced by the Subcommittee were informed by members' expertise, as well as numerous consultations with community leaders, innovators, and families, in town halls and listening sessions around the country.†

Accomplishments

Encouraging Local Financial Capability Councils. The chief accomplishment of the Underserved and Community Empowerment Subcommittee has been to inspire and encourage local financial capability councils across the country. These councils are designed to coordinate the financial education programs provided by both the public and private sector. Typically led by mayors, these councils run at low-or no-cost and appoint local stakeholders with an interest in financial capability. These stakeholders are typically "C-Suite" leaders from financial institutions, schools, faith-based organizations, and the local government. They come together to identify what works, what doesn't, and what needs to be expanded upon to increase the financial capability of their community.

To date, 110 communities have expressed a written commitment to create such a council and most estimate a timeline of completion around three months. For example, in the District of Columbia the Local Financial Literacy Council is already operational and held a Town Hall on November 28, 2012. As a result of this Town Hall, that same day, the DC State Board of Education

† Subcommittee members hosted or participated in listening sessions, town hall meetings, and other gatherings, including the following: Federal Reserve Bank of Chicago Financial Literacy and Education Summit, Chicago, IL; Indianapolis Campaign for Financial Fitness, Indianapolis, IN; Center for Financial Services Innovation; Society for Financial Education and Professional Development's 4th Annual Financial Literacy Leadership Conference, Washington, DC; listening sessions in Atlanta, GA; Oxon Hill, MD; Minneapolis, MN, and San Antonio, TX; Federal Reserve Bank of St Louis' Innovations in Savings and Financial Education Forum, St Louis, MO; Step Up Savannah, Savannah, GA; Cities for Financial Empowerment Coalition, Los Angeles, CA; Council for Native Hawaiian Advancement, Honolulu, Hawaii; and National Congress of American Indians, Sacramento, CA.

voted unanimously to require all public high school students to take a financial literacy course before graduation.

The Subcommittee would not have been able to assist the efforts of these mayors had it not been for the work of the Partnership Subcommittee, which prepared a resource guide that has provided structural guidance to those developing councils.

Acknowledging the importance of financial capability in emergency preparedness and recovery. A second key accomplishment of the Subcommittee was recommending to the President that the Federal Emergency Management Agency be integrated into the Financial Literacy Education Commission.

In the face of a disaster, financial preparedness is of paramount importance. The foresight to integrate these efforts came from the Chairman of the Subcommittee prior to the tragic events of Hurricane Sandy. Since making the recommendation, the importance of this integration has become self-evident.

Promoting existing resources on student aid to more Americans. The third major accomplishment of the Subcommittee was its recommendation that the federal government establish an awareness campaign, that leads the American people to www.studentaid.gov as the one stop resource for students and families to increase college affordability and reduce student loan debt.

Summaries of the full recommendations are found in Appendix B.

Recommendations and Accomplishments Research and Evaluation Subcommittee

Purpose

Ongoing and rigorous financial education and financial access research and evaluation will lead to better understanding of the barriers to widespread financial capability, and of the effectiveness of interventions that aim to address them. This Subcommittee focused on learning about the findings of existing research, identifying research gaps, articulating needs within the program evaluation framework, and providing a foundation of understanding for those interested in financial capability education, policy, regulation and context. In building upon what is known, the Subcommittee substantiated the need going forward to continually test the ideas with greatest potential to accompany ongoing research. The Subcommittee also provided insight and guidance to the other Subcommittees to ensure that their recommendations were research-based and incorporate appropriate success metrics.

Accomplishments

Research-Based Framework. The Subcommittee crystallized the wisdom and findings of researchers, practitioners and policy-makers into the framework for financial capability supported by the three legs of financial education, regulation and consumer protection, and thoughtful design of options (choice architecture).

Data Collection and Sharing. The subcommittee encouraged and supported the second wave of the FINRA Investor Education Foundation's extensive National Financial Capability Survey; and U.S. participation in the international benchmarking Programme for International Student Assessment study of the financial capability of 15-year-olds globally.

Research Gaps. Based on its extensive review of existing research and the inventory of research priorities as reported through Subcommittee discussions, the Subcommittee identified topics of potential relevance to people's financial capability for future research and testing. In the area of context and delivery, more study is needed on the use of technology, employer engagement, integration of financial products and education, the role of social learning and how to influence people's social networks, the role of cognitive load and attention limitations, and the role of diminished capacity (such as, as a function of depletion). Additional research and testing is recommended for areas related to personalization, such as gender, age and other relevant demographics, and personal characteristics such as the propensity to plan , confidence, and access to unbiased information.

National Research Priorities. Subcommittee members joined the Financial Literacy and Education Commission working group in September 2011 to discuss national research priorities, resulting in identification of three areas of focus: delivery and access; evaluation; and risk. The Commission's resulting report, 2012 Research Priorities and Research Questions, which was endorsed by the full Council, is intended to broadly guide research and research funding in the field in nine key areas:

- **Evaluate Successful Financial Education Delivery:** Evaluate the delivery of financial education for youth and adults in order to identify effective approaches, delivery channels, and other factors (such as the interaction of knowledge, products, and behaviors) that enhance effectiveness.

- **Identify Optimal Strategy Combinations**: Identify optimal combinations of financial information, advice, regulation, disclosure, and delivery mechanisms, including default options, and their impact on starting and maintaining positive financial habits.
- **Conduct Longitudinal Assessments**: Employ longitudinal data to evaluate the effectiveness of core competencies on behavior and financial well-being over time.
- **Identify Key Measures of Success**: Identify, evaluate, and build consensus on "key metrics" for financial education/capability, including measures of knowledge, behavior, and well-being.
- **Evaluate Interactions between Education and Product Design**: Identify and evaluate the relationship between financial education and access to and design of high quality financial products.
- **Assess the Impact of Business Cycles**: Assess the role of business cycles and economic and financial context in individuals' financial decision making.
- **Explore the Impacts of Risk and Financial Shocks**: Ascertain how risk and uncertainty, including economic and other shocks, alter risk exposure and risk management choices both at the consumer and community levels.
- **Identify Local, State, and Federal "Scalable" Opportunities**: Identify opportunities and roles for local, state, and federal governments as scalable platforms for financial capability.
- **Leverage Synergies with Other Subject Areas**: Identify and evaluate potential synergies between educational programs targeting financial capability and those targeting physical and mental health.

Summaries of the full recommendations are found in Appendix B.

Appendix A: Council Subcommittees Membership as of December 2012

Underserved and Community Empowerment
Chair: John Bryant
Members:
Ted Beck
Arty Arteaga

Janie Barrera
Sherry Salway Black
Samuel Jackson
Marc Morial
Carrie Schwab-Pomerantz
Eldar Shafir
John Rogers (ex-officio member)
Ken Wade

Research and Evaluation
Chair: Ted Beck

Members:
Rick Ketchum
John Rogers (ex-officio member)
Eldar Shafir
Ken Wade

Partnerships
Chair: Carrie Schwab-Pomerantz

Members:
Arty Arteaga
John Bryant
Rick Ketchum
Barry Rand
John Rogers (ex-officio member)
Amy Rosen

Youth
Chair: Amy Rosen
Members:
Ted Beck
Sherry Salway Black
John Bryant
Samuel Jackson
Beth Kobliner
John Rogers (ex-officio member)

Appendix B. Recommendations as Approved by the Council and Status as of January 29, 2013

Theme	Recommendation	Status
Youth	That the President champion this Money as You Learn approach and instruct the Financial Literacy and Education Commission, and its member agencies, to take all possible steps to advance it. The Council also calls on national financial literacy organizations and their state and local partners to embrace Money as You Learn and to build an enduring initiative that will improve the financial capability of our young people for years to come.	Money as You Learn initiative underway in the private sector through collaboration with developers and leaders of the Common Core State Standards, Jump$tart, Council for Economic Education, teachers and other experts. A website, www.MoneyAsYouLearn.org, is currently in development. The Financial Literacy and Education Commission, led by the Department of the Treasury, is considering how best to support this effort given resources available, and agency missions and authorities.
Youth, Communities and Families	That the President encourage federal agencies, through Executive Order, to promote and utilize Money as You Grow as one tool to improve the financial capability of America's youth.	To date, more than 500,000 people have visited www.MoneyAsYouGrow.org, and the site continues to attract approximately 10,000 new visitors each week. The Department of the Treasury will consult with Department of Education and other agencies, along with outside stakeholders, to determine best approach to implement given resources available, and agency missions and authorities.
Youth, Communities and Families	That the President encourage federal agencies, through Executive Order, to promote and utilize Money as You Grow as one tool to improve the financial capability of America's youth.	To date, more than 500,000 people have visited www.MoneyAsYouGrow.org, and the site continues to attract approximately 10,000 new visitors each week. The Department of the

(Continued)

Theme	Recommendation	Status
		Treasury will consult with Department of Education and other agencies, along with outside stakeholders, to determine best approach to implement given resources available, and agency missions and authorities.
Youth	That the United States participate in the financial literacy module of the Program for International Student Assessment (PISA) that measures 15-year-old students' reading, mathematics, and science literacy and other competencies.	The PISA Financial Literacy Module was implemented in 2012.
Youth	That the Department of Education, in collaboration with the Department of Treasury and the Financial Literacy and Education Commission, actively participate in the international PISA study through the 2015 cycle.	The Department of Education is planning to implement this recommendation.
Communities and Families	That the federal government encourage the creation of operational councils at the state, local and tribal level to help improve the financial capability of citizens.	An estimated 110 councils are being formed, according to the National Conference of Black Mayors, with more possible. The "Creating Financially Capable Communities" resource guide was developed to help localized efforts and is available at http://www. treasury.gov/resource-center/financial education /Documents/Local%20Guide%20- %20Creating%20 Financially%20Capable%20Co mmunities.pdf

Theme	Recommendation	Status
		The Department of the Treasury is reviewing and considering other ways to support implementation of this recommendation, given resources, mission and authorities.
Communities and Families, Youth	That the President direct the appropriate federal agencies led by the U.S. Department of Education's Federal Student Aid Office, to launch an awareness campaign that leads the American people to www.studentaid.gov as the one stop resource for students and families to increase college affordability and reduce student loan debt, which may be entitled Know Before You Apply.	The Department of Education, will consult with other members of the Financial Literacy and Education Commission and other partners regarding implementing this recommendation.
Communities and Families	That the Department of the Treasury evaluate the merit of the Roth at Birth concept, intended to encourage families to begin early savings for their children, and consider whether legislation to allow children to use their immediate families' earned income to start a savings program would be advisable.	The Department of the Treasury will consider as part of a larger assessment of tax policy.
Communities and Families	That the President and the Secretary of the Treasury integrate the field of emergency financial and economic disaster preparedness response and recovery into the broader financial capability efforts of the federal government, and invite the Federal Emergency	The Department of the Treasury is working with the White House to implement the recommendation.

(Continued)

Theme	Recommendation	Status
	Management Administration to be a part of the Financial Literacy and Education Commission.	
Communities and Families	That the Department of the Treasury hold a challenge to the private sector to create applications for mobile devices that promote financial capability and financial access.	The Department of the Treasury implemented the MyMoney App Up Challenge, in partnership with two national non-profit organizations. The top five app design finalists were selected to receive $25,000 in prizes. These five submissions were selected as winners from more than 300 ideas submitted.
Workplace	That the President encourage private sector, nonprofit and state/tribal/local government employers to make it a priority to improve the financial capability of their employees, and that the President support that effort by: 1) Designating the Department of Labor and the Small Business	the the developed and is publicly available at The resource "Financial Capability at Work" was http://www.treasury.gov/resour cecenter/ financialeducation/ Documents/PACFC%20Financ ial%20C apability%20at%20Work.pdf.
	Administration as the federal government's lead agencies in the effort to expand workplace financial education; 2) Directing the Department of Labor and the Small Business Administration to dedicate staff and resources to the dissemination and promotion of "Financial Capability at Work: A Strategic Framework to Guide Employers," a PACFCproduced guide and resource document to help	The Department of the Treasury is working with the Department of Labor, the Small Business Administration, and others to develop approaches to implementing key aspects of the recommendation and that ensure necessary consumer protections in place, consistent with ir statutory mission and authority as well as ir resource priorities

Theme	Recommendation	Status
	employers provide quality financial capability information and programs to their employees; and 3) Directing the Department of Labor to revisit Interpretive Bulletin 96-1 ("Participant Investment Education") to provide more clarity to employers on the range of financial education topics and activities that are permissible under the Employee Retirement Income Security Act (ERISA) of 1974.	
Workplace	That the Department of the Treasury support a newly-created private-sector award program, the Workplace Leaders in Financial Education (WLIFE) Awards, which recognizes employers that provide outstanding financial education to their employees.	The Department of the Treasury recognized the 2011 winners of the WLIFE award at an event in January 2012.
Workplace	That the federal government develop tools to increase financial capability resources for federal employees, such as bringing financial advisors to the workplace for use by employees. Those tools will then be used to set an example for the private sector and other employers to adopt mechanisms that encourage financial capability among their own employees.	The Office of Personnel Management is working on enhanced tools and resources to promote the financial capability of federal employees.
Research and Evaluation	That the Department of Treasury in collaboration with Financial Literacy and Education Commission explore the possibility of building and sustaining a	The Department of Treasury will consult with the Department of Education and other agencies to assess this recommendation.

(Continued)

Theme	Recommendation	Status
	Doing What Works website for financial capability that is modeled after the Department of Education's Doing What Works initiative, subject to the resources available to support such a website.	
Research and Evaluation	That the Department of the Treasury and other relevant agencies consult on the development, fielding and dissemination of data from a second wave of the National Financial Capability Study (conducted by the FINRA Investor Education Foundation) to be conducted 2012.	The Department of the Treasury, along with other federal agencies worked with the FINRA Investor Education Foundation in its 2012 implementation of the National Financial Capability Study.
Research and Evaluation	That the federal government support development and dissemination of universal outcome metrics, program evaluation standards and financial education research standards to improve the quality and effectiveness of programs and research and help educators choose programs best suited for their learners' objectives.	The Financial Literacy and Education Commission released a set of Research Priorities and Questions and is continuing to work individually and together on promoting research and evaluation in the financial capability field.

APPENDIX C: MONEY AS YOU LEARN

The President's Advisory Council on Financial Capability calls for a new initiative – *Money as You Learn* -- to integrate important aspects personal finance into English language arts and mathematics teaching as well as into other classes and afterschool programs, in order to reach more students throughout their schooling.

This approach can strengthen learning of those subjects as well as expose all students to knowledge and skills they need to become financially capable young adults. At the same time, the Council continues to urge states and school districts to also provide high quality personal finance classes for their students.

The Council recommends that the President champion this *Money as You Learn* approach and instruct the Financial Literacy and Education Commission, and its member agencies, to take all possible steps to advance it. The Council also calls on national financial literacy organizations and their state and local partners to embrace *Money as You Learn* and to build an enduring initiative that will improve the financial capability of our young people for years to come.

This call is timely. Forty-five states and the District of Columbia have recently adopted the Common Core State Standards in mathematics and English language arts. These new standards, whose development was led by the States, provide a consistent, clear understanding of the academic knowledge and skills students are expected to learn in order to be prepared for success in college and careers.

The transition to the Common Core State Standards provides a once-in-a-generation opportunity to effectively integrate personal finance into the K-12 curriculum in ways that provide students with essential personal finance understanding and skills. In addition, teaching of the Common Core is strengthened by providing real-world, practical contexts and applications that are relevant, engaging and meaningful to students.

Educators across the nation are eager for Common Core-aligned curriculum materials that capture the key shifts embedded in the standards. The time is therefore ripe for identifying texts, creating mathematical tasks, and designing lessons that inform students at all grade levels about key ideas regarding personal finance that are grounded in the Common Core standards. There is also the opportunity for states to model the value of this approach by routinely including items in their assessments that take advantage of core personal finance concepts and contexts.

Supporting educators in making this a reality requires the following actions: (1) map where essential personal finance knowledge and skills can be integrated into the Common Core State Standards; (2) develop tools for educators to integrate personal finance into teaching of the Common Core State Standards; (3) align existing personal finance programs with the Common Core State Standards; and (4) invest in research and evaluation on effective teaching and learning of personal finance.

Text Box A. Mapping of Financial Literacy Big Ideas and the Common Core Mathematics Standards at Grade 6

The horizontal column identifies critical aspects in the area of personal finance that are elements of foundational understanding that would lead students to an action or a higher level of function. For example, understanding compound interest leads to saving, understanding the importance of starting early, and more effective debt management. Similarly, understanding inflation leads to the ability to mitigate its effects with respect to investments, assumption of debt, and purchasing decisions. The vertical column identifies the Grade 6 Common Core Mathematics Standards where financial literacy concepts and skills can provide appropriate context and content for teaching the standard. Eventually, each square of the grid will contain mathematical tasks and other materials. At www.moneyasyougrow.org, educators will be able to search by grade, by mathematics and English standards, and by financial literacy content for tasks, texts, lesson plans and other tools.

	Financial Literacy Big Ideas										
Common Core Math Cluster/ Standard for Grade 6	Compound Interest	Oppor-tunity Cost	Value of Education	What is Money	Cost/ Benefit Analysis	Debt	Risk	Setting Goals	Delayed Gratification	Scarcity	Inflation
6.RP.3 Use ratio and rate reasoning to solve real-world problems											
6.NS.5 Positive/negative #s											
6.EE.1 Write/evaluate using whole # exponents											
6 EE.2 Write, read, evaluate expressions where letters stand for #s											
6.EE.9 Use variables to represent 2 qty, ind./dep. Variables											
6.SP Stat and Prob.											

As described below, collaboration among the Council, developers and leaders of the Common Core State Standards, financial education experts, and extraordinary teachers has already spurred progress on the first two action items leading to the forthcoming website, www.moneyasyoulearn.org, with tools for educators.

Mapping how essential personal finance knowledge and skills can be integrated into the Common Core State Standards

The President's Council has catalyzed a mapping between essential personal finance concepts and skills and the Common Core State Standards that will show where personal finance can provide appropriate context and content for mathematics and English language arts teaching. The Council urges the financial literacy field to look towards this forthcoming mapping as a resource for action. A sample of the mathematics mapping is in text box A.

Of course, not all important personal finance content can be appropriately integrated into the Common Core, and vice versa. Thus, this mapping will not cover the full scope of existing personal finance standards and the Council urges states and school districts to also provide high quality personal finance classes for their students.

Moreover, as the Council considered the important personal finance concepts that can be integrated into the Common Core, the effort has revealed an underlying challenge – the multiple personal finance standards that have been promulgated by national organizations as well as by various states. Developing high quality programs and curriculum materials, engaging teachers in professional learning to enhance the teaching of personal finance, and evaluating the effectiveness of financial literacy initiatives are all more difficult when there are multiple sets of standards with differences in content, terminology, sequencing and focus. The field will benefit from personal finance experts coalescing around one set of standards grounded in the best available evidence on what young adults need to know to be able to effectively manage their own financial lives. The Council urges leaders in the financial literacy field to take the necessary steps in this direction.

Tools for Educators

Educators will benefit from concrete guidance and tools to support their work of appropriately integrating financial literacy and the Common Core. The Council has encouraged the development of mathematics tasks and identification of non-fiction texts that enhance the teaching of the Common

Core through important, real-world personal finance applications, skills and issues. Collaboration among developers and leaders of the Common Core State Standards, Jump$tart Coalition for Personal Financial Literacy, Council for Economic Education, and *Money as You Grow,* as well as classroom teachers and other experts from around the nation, will ensure that these instructional materials reflect the rigor and important shifts of the new standards as well as financial literacy content that all students should master. For example, mathematical tasks may call for students to apply their mathematical knowledge in important, real world contexts such as budgeting, understanding compound interest, or assessing risk. Similarly, non-fiction texts such as a pay stub or cell phone bill or writing on topics such as the value of setting financial goals or the roots of the mortgage crisis can be tools for deepening student ability to understand and use complex texts in English language arts lessons.

Text Box B. Example Mathematics Task

This task addresses the second grade mathematics standard addressing solving word problems with monetary units and the important financial literacy concept of opportunity cost.

Susan wanted to make a birthday card for her best friend but needed some art supplies. She emptied her piggy bank and found 1 quarter, 5 dimes, 3 nickels, and 8 pennies.

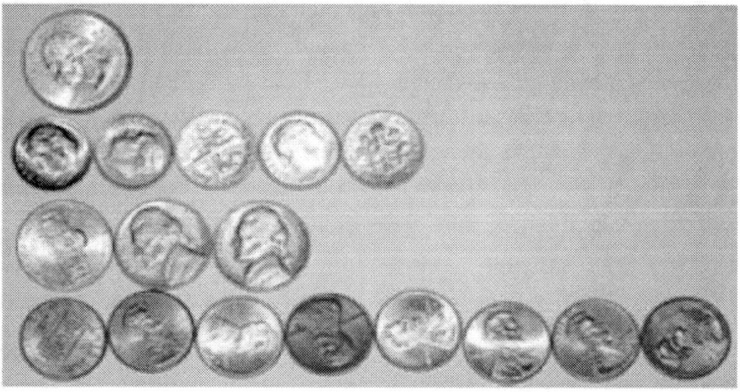

How much money did Susan find in her piggy bank? Show or explain how you know.

Susan went to the store with her mother and saw a pack of stickers for 35¢ and a glitter pen for 60¢. Does Susan have enough money to buy both items to make her birthday card? Show or explain how you know.

While Susan was at the store, she saw a ring that she would like to have herself. The ring costs 45¢. Can she still buy one or both of the other items?

Commentary:

The purpose of this task is to address the concept of opportunity cost through a real world context involving money. In economics, resources are limited, but our wants are unlimited. Therefore, choices must be made. Every choice involves a cost. Your **opportunity cost** is the value of the next best alternative you gave up, or did not choose, when making a decision. To learn more about opportunity cost, visit www.econedLink.org.

Prior to this task, it would be helpful for students to have a basic understanding of decision making. The teacher can hold a discussion with students regarding opportunity cost by asking them what Susan is giving up if she buys the ring. Responses might include 45¢, the glitter pen, the stickers, or even the ability to make the card the way she wanted to. At this point, a grade-appropriate definition/explanation of opportunity cost could be discussed.

Second graders are ready to think about the ideas presented by the task, but depending on their reading level, the questions might be best presented verbally by the teacher before students are asked to work independently or in groups. Note that the numbers were carefully chosen so that the addition and subtraction they do is within 100 (2.OA.1) and the steps shown in finding these sums and differences reflect strategies based on place value and properties of operations (2.NBT.5). Also, students in second grade are asked to skip-count by 5's, 10's, and 100's (see 2.NBT.2) but have not yet formalized these ideas in terms of the concept of multiplication. As a result, the solution given shows a skip-counting approach; if this task were given to third graders, they would be more likely to naturally formulate the solution in terms of multiplication. This task is part of a set collaboratively developed by *Money as You Learn* and Illustrative Mathematics, which provides guidance to states, assessment consortia, testing companies, and curriculum developers by illustrating the range and types of mathematical work that students experience in a faithful implementation of the Common Core State Standards, and by publishing other tools that support implementation of the standards.

The task (and accompanying solutions) is available at www.illustrativemathematics.org as well as the forthcoming www.moneyasyoulearn.org.

While initial work has begun, much more remains to be done to develop and identify outstanding materials and lessons and provide supports for teachers to enable them to effectively integrate financial literacy into their teaching.

The Council calls on leaders of the financial literacy community -- including but not limited to Jump$tart Coalition for Personal Financial Literacy, Council for Economic Education, and members of the Financial Literacy and Education Commission -- to expand on this *Money as You Learn* effort and develop effective guidance and instructional materials, and an easy-to-use, high quality national website for personal finance resources linked to the Common Core that is shared with educators nationwide.

Align existing personal finance programs with the demands of Common Core State Standards Leaders in the financial literacy field will benefit from moving quickly to review and where appropriate revise existing personal finance programs so that they are consistent with and support attainment of the Common Core.

This review should be done by state and local education leaders responsible for personal finance programs, financial literacy organizations that implement programs, and by the federal agencies that comprise the Financial Literacy and Education Commission and provide financial literacy resources. This review and appropriate updating of programs and curriculum should be done for personal finance and entrepreneurship classes, for other classes such as economics, social studies, career and technical education, and for after-school programs.

Given the distance many of our nation's students need to travel to be fully prepared for college and careers, it is critically important that every minute of instruction is well used. The more personal finance programs can demonstrably support students attaining the mathematical and literacy competencies called for in the Common Core, as well as the skills of problem-solving, research and careful reading and analysis that cut across all subject areas, the more likely it is that there will be time in the school day and after-school for students to have access to high quality personal finance content – as well as the quantitative and literacy skills they will need to be financially capable adults.

Investment in Research and Evaluation

Consistent with the Council's research recommendations, in the area of financial education the Council urges the President to direct federal investment in research and evaluation in order to identify the most effective ways to help young people build the knowledge, skills and dispositions needed to be financially capable adults. While it is essential to act now based on what we know today, it is also essential to invest more in research on financial education to better understand instructional approaches that have impact on student's personal finance knowledge and behaviors.

Several types of research are needed. First, using insights developed in the field of financial education and behavioral economics, more basic research needs to be done to identify the types of school-based learning experiences that impact later financial decisions, and then work needs to be done to embed those findings into school programs and test out their efficacy. Second, the work described above to integrate the teaching of personal finance into the Common Core should be tested and evaluated and improved over time. Third, more evaluations of existing, large-scale personal finance programs should be conducted and the results made widely accessible. Most importantly, those who develop personal finance programs and those who carry them out in schools should demand and hold themselves accountable to evidence – independent evaluations of what works, program data on growth in student knowledge and skills, and longitudinal data on student financial decision-making.

Doing high quality research and evaluation and building the capacity of organizations to better use evidence and data, requires resources of many sorts, including significant funding. Private and non-profit organizations supporting personal finance should increase their investment in research and use of evidence.

However, it is critical that the federal government commit to a significant and long-term program of funding in this area that allows for the development and aggregation of knowledge over multiple studies, in multiple contexts, in multiple areas of research and evaluation. The federal government is best positioned to make this essential sustained investment and this is a high leverage role for the federal government since increased knowledge about what works can inform and enrich the future actions of all those who seek to increase our young people's financial capability. Research on financial literacy proposed by the Financial Literacy and Education Commission should reflect the funding and research recommendations of the Council.

APPENDIX D: ACKNOWLEDGMENTS

The members of the President's Advisory Council wish to thank the following individuals for sharing their experience, insights, and opinions and for their support of the Council's efforts:

Current and Past Staff of Council Organizations

Jon	Dauphine	AARP
Jean	Setzfand	AARP
Celina	Pena	ACCION Texas, Inc.
Connie	Moran	Ariel Investments
Ellen	Chube	Ariel Investments
Amar	Parikh	Ariel Investments
Bob	Solomon	Ariel Investments
Sarah	Courteau	Beth Kobliner Company
Harold	Kobliner	Beth Kobliner Company
Shirley	Kobliner	Beth Kobliner Company
Leslie	Schnur	Beth Kobliner Company
Kristine	Dixon	Charles Schwab
Michael	Townsend	Charles Schwab
Jennifer	Kenney	Defense Credit Union Council
Beth	Merlo	Defense Credit Union Council
Judy	Wurtzel	Education Policy Consultant
Christine	Kieffer	Financial Industry Regulatory Authority
Gary	Mottola	Financial Industry Regulatory Authority
Gerri	Walsh	Financial Industry Regulatory Authority
Billy	Hensley	National Endowment for Financial Education
Brent	Neiser	National Endowment for Financial Education
Patricia	Seaman	National Endowment for Financial Education
Susan	Sharkey	National Endowment for Financial Education
Ainsley	O'Connell	Network for Teaching Entrepreneurship
Christine	Poorman	Network for Teaching Entrepreneurship
Rachel	Doff	Operation HOPE

Mary	Hagerty	Operation HOPE
Alaina	Reaves	Operation HOPE
Christian	Robinson	Operation HOPE
Jena	Roscoe	Operation HOPE
Lance	Triggs	Operation HOPE
Katherine	Trujillo	Operation HOPE
Lucas	Turner-Owens	Operation HOPE

Consumer Financial Protection Bureau (current and former staff)

Richard	Cordray	Director
Elizabeth	Warren	Special Advisor to the Secretary of the Treasury
Gail	Hillebrand	Associate Director
Eleni	Constantine	Deputy Associate Director
Camille	Busette	Assistant Director, Office of Financial Education
Holly	Petraeus	Assistant Director, Office of Service Member Affairs
Dubis	Correal	Strategic Partnerships and Outreach Coordinator
Matthew	Pippin	Policy Analyst, Consumer Education and Engagement

Department of Education (current and former staff)

Arne	Duncan	Secretary
Joanne	Weiss	Chief of Staff
David	Soo	Senior Advisor and Policy Analyst
Jo	Anderson	Senior Advisor
Phil	Martin	Senior Advisor
Karen	Gross	Senior Advisor

Other Governmental Agencies

Susan	Shockey	US Department of Agriculture
Robert	Mooney	Federal Deposit Insurance Corporation
Tonya	Sweat	National Credit Union Administration
Denise	Murray	Office of the Comptroller of the Currency
Barry	Wides	Office of the Comptroller of the Currency
Ray	Kirk	Office of Personnel Management
Sarah	MacDougall	Securities and Exchange Commission
David	Weaver	Social Security Administration

The White House (current and former staff)

William	Daley	Chief of Staff
Valerie	Jarrett	Senior Advisor to the President
Matt	Flavin	Former Director of Veterans and Wounded Warrior Policy
Pete	Rouse	Counselor to the President
Gene	Sperling	Director of the National Economic Council and Assistant to the President for Economic Policy
Alan	Krueger	Chairman, Council of Economic Advisors
Macon	Phillips	Director of New Media
Greg	Nelson	Deputy Director, Office of Public Engagement
Thomas	Kalil	Special Assistant to the President for Economic Policy
John	Oxtoby	Intergovernmental Affairs Staff Assistant
Doug	Rand	Senior Policy Advisor, Office of Science and Technology Policy
Racquel	Russell	Deputy Assistant to the President for Urban Affairs and Economic Mobility
Zakiya	Smith	Senior Advisor for Education, Domestic Policy Council
Constance Steinkuehler	Squire	Senior Policy Analyst, Office of Science and Technology Policy
Michael	Strautmanis	Deputy Assistant to the President and Counselor for Strategic Engagement to the Senior Advisor
Diana	Zarzuelo	Policy Assistant on Urban Policy and Mobility Opportunity

Department of the Treasury (current and former staff)

Neal	Wolin	Acting Secretary
Mary	Miller	Under Secretary for Domestic Finance
Cyrus	Amir-Mokri	Assistant Secretary for Financial Institutions
Michael	Barr	Former Assistant Secretary for Financial Institutions
Don	Graves	Deputy Assistant Secretary for Small Business, Housing and Community Development
Melissa	Koide	Deputy Assistant Secretary, Office of Consumer Policy and Executive Director, President's Advisory Council on Financial Capability
Louisa	Quittman	Director, Office of Financial Education
Sophie	Raseman	Director for Smart Disclosure
Joshua	Wright	Former Acting Director, Office of Financial Access

Other Organizations

William	Porro	ACCESS Miami
Michael	Cohen	Achieve
Kay	Forgione	Achieve
George	Barany	America Saves
Barbara	Kontje	American Express
Stephanie	Myers	American Federation of Teachers
Randi	Weingarten	American Federation of Teachers
Melora	Heavey	American Institute of Certified Public Accountants
Ken	McDonnell	American Savings Education Council
Eric	Sparks	American School Counselor Association
Peggy	Powell	America's Credit Union Museum
Suzanne	Curren	Andrews Federal Credit Union
Lewis	Mandell	Aspen Institute
Lisa	Mensah	Aspen Institute

(Continued)

Rachel	Payne	Association for Library Service to Children
Aimee	Strittmatter	Association for Library Service to Children
Frances	Veit	Association for Library Service to Children
Tisha	Wallace	Belvoir Federal Credit Union
Jeanne	Hogarth	Board of Governors of the Federal Reserve System
Erica	Swerdlow	Burston Marsteller
Suzanne	Matthews	Center for Financial and Economic Education, Westchester Community College
John	Pelletier	Center for Financial Literacy, Champlain College
Michael	Collins	Center for Financial Security, University of Wisconsin
Jennifer	Tescher	Center for Financial Services Innovation
Margaret	Sherraden	Center for Social Development, Washington University
Linda	Rosen	Change the Equation
Stephanie	Neely	City of Chicago
Jennifer	Cheatham	Chicago Public Schools
Hector	Gonzalez	Chicago Public Schools
Martin	Moe	Chicago Public Schools
David	Vitale	Chicago Public Schools
David	Coleman	College Board
Brenda	Barr	Colorado Department of Education
Adrian	Franco	Columbia University
Sue	Sporte	Consortium on Chicago School Research
George	Barany	Consumer Federation of America
Ida	Rademacher	Corporation for Enterprise Development
Carl	Rist	Corporation for Enterprise Development

Nan	Morrison	Council of Economic Education
David	Pook	Derryfield School
David	Nelms	Discover Financial
Leslie	Sutton	Discover Financial
Matthew	Towson	Discover Financial
Tim	Flacke	Doorways to Dreams Fund
John	Doyle	Doyle McDonald
Valerie	Klein	Drexel University
Suyeon	Kim	Edulender
Dallas	Salisbury	Employee Benefit Research Institute
Catherine	Niehaus	E-Trade Financial Corp.
Mark	Kantrowitz	Fastweb.com and Finaid.org
Richard	Oliver	Federal Reserve Bank of Atlanta
Tiffany	Butler	Federal Reserve Bank of Chicago
Richard	Todd	Federal Reserve Bank of Minneapolis
Tony	Davis	Federal Reserve Bank of New York
Kris	Bertelsen	Federal Reserve Bank of St. Louis
Ray	Boshara	Federal Reserve Bank of St. Louis
Mary	Suiter	Federal Reserve Bank of St. Louis
Steve	Bartlett	Financial Services Roundtable
Judy	Chapa	Financial Services Roundtable
Lisa	McLain-Sharp	Fort McCoy Army Community Service
Jim	Clifton	Gallup Corporation
Jason	Milton	Gallup Corporation
Annamaria	Lusardi	George Washington University School of Business
Maura	Donlan	Greer, Margolis, Mitchell, Burns
David	Mitchell	Greer, Margolis, Mitchell, Burns
Jaime	Zapata	Greer, Margolis, Mitchell, Burns
Matt	Fellowes	HelloWallet
Bill	McCallum	Illustrative Mathematics
Kristin	Umland	Illustrative Mathematics
Karli	Simmons	Indiana Securities Division
Winnie	Ballard	Indianapolis Campaign for Financial Fitness
Cheryl	Oldham	Institute for a Competitive Workforce
Lois	Vitt	Institute for Socio-Financial Studies

(Continued)

Wes	Hall	Institute for Student Empowerment
Tahira	Hira	Iowa State University
Jim	Hedemark	Jump$tart Coalition of Rhode Island
Laura	Levine	JumpStart Coalition for Personal Financial Literacy
Jack	Kosakowski	Junior Achievement USA
Ruben	Fernandez	LadderUp
Luis	Pastor	Latino Community Credit Union
Paul	Cloutier	Levanto Financial
Jeanine	Moore	Long Neck Elementary
Luke	Rhine	Maryland Department of Education
David	Carroll	McDonald's Corporation
Bridget	Coffing	McDonald's Corporation
Richard	Floersch	McDonald's Corporation
Steven	Hilton	McDonald's Corporation
Artemis Bakopoulos	Hiss	McDonald's Corporation
Mary	Viola	McDonald's Corporation
Kathy	Jacoby	MetLife
Jason	Saul	Mission Measurement
Margaret	Libby	Mission SF Community Financial Center
Kathy	Griffin	MoneyU.com
Kelvin	Boston	Moneywise
Andrea	Ingram	Museum of Science and Industry
Deb	Bongiorno	National Association of Elementary School Principals
Megan	McClean	National Association of Financial Aid Administrators
Robin	Gemeinhardt	National Association of Personal Financial Advisors
Karen	Nystrom	National Association of Personal Financial Advisors
Vanessa	Williams	National Congress of Black Mayors
Lois	Kitsch	National Credit Union Foundation
Bucky	Sebastian	National Credit Union Foundation

Andrea	Prejean	National Education Association
Cliff	Rosenthal	National Federation of Community Development Credit Unions
Mary	King	National Parent Teacher Association
Debbie	Arnold	Near Field Communication Forum
Michael	Ehrlich	New Jersey Institute of Technology
Jonathan	Mintz	City of New York
Michelle	Greene	New York Stock Exchange Euronext, Inc.
Richard	Arum	New York University
Jeff	Nelhaus	Partnership for Assessment of Readiness for College and Careers
Mary	Rosenkrans	Pennsylvania Office of Financial Education
Lisa	Krueger	Princeton High School
Barbara	Macikas	Public Library Association
Brian	Page	Reading Community City School
Rebecca	Reed	Red Clay Consolidated School District
Jose	Cisneros	City of San Francisco
Priya	Haji	Save Up
Rachel	Goldman	Shepherd Elementary School
Margaret	Monsour	Smart Investing @ Your Library
Shelbi	Cole	Smarter Balanced Assessment Consortium
Sandy	Boost	Society for Human Resource Management
Janet	Parker	Society for Human Resource Management
Daniel	Dodd-Ramirez	Step Up Savannah
Robyn	Wainner	Step Up Savannah
Deb	Figart	Stockton Center for Economic and Financial Literacy
Sue	Pimentel	Student Achievement Partners
Jason	Zimba	Student Achievement Partners
Rob	Savage	Taco Bell Corporation
Richard	Enswiller	Texas Credit Union League
Betsy	Palmer	TIAA-CREF

(Continued)

Punam Anand	Keller	Tuck School of Business, Dartmouth College
Tom	Donohue	US Chamber of Commerce
Holly	Kuzmich	US Chamber of Commerce
Michael	Staten	University of Arizona
Richard	Thaler	University of Chicago
Julia	Heath	University of Cincinnati
John	Lynch	University of Colorado Boulder
William	Walstad	University of Nebraska–Lincoln
Claudia	Kerbel	University of Rhode Island
Karen	Holden	University of Wisconsin-Madison
Chuck	Kalish	University of Wisconsin-Madison
Tom	Watjean	UNUM
Erin	Boettcher	Wilbur Elementary School
Kristen	McDaniel	Wisconsin Department of Public Instruction
David	Mancl	Wisconsin Office of Financial Education
Cindy	Hounsell	Women's Institute for a Secure Retirement
Sabrina	Lamb	World of Money
Martha	Staten	

APPENDIX E: ENDNOTES

[1] Lusardi, A. and Mitchell, O. (2009) How Ordinary Consumers Make Complex Economic Decisions: Financial Literacy and Retirement Readiness. *National Bureau of Economic Research.*

[2] FINRA Investor Education Foundation, National Survey of the Financial Capability Study, 2009. http://www.finrafoundation/capability

[3] Xiao, J., Collins, M., Ford, M., Keller, P., Kim, J., Robles, B. (2010). "A Review of Financial Behavior Research: Implications for Financial Education" National Endowment for Financial Education Quarter Century Project, http://www.nefe.org/Portals/0/WhatWe Provide/PrimaryResearch/PDF/TheQtrCenturyProject_Theme 2_FinancialBehaviorsandMotivators.pdf

[4] Boshara, R., Gannon, J., Mandell, L., Phillips, J.W.R., Sass, S. (2010) "Consumer Trends in the Public, Private, and Nonprofit Sector" National Endowment for Financial Education

Quarter Century Project. http://www.nefe.org/Portals/0/WhatWeProvide/Primary Research /PDF/TheQtrCenturyProject_Theme 4_ConsumerTrendsInThePublic.pdf

[5] National Endowment for Financial Education, (2011). "How Americans Are Using Their Tax Refunds: Paying Down Debt, Saving Priorities Among Those Who Withhold More." http://www.nefe.org/press-room/news/tax-refund-2011.aspx

[6] Iyengar, S. S., & Lepper, M. (2000) When Choice is Demotivating: Can One Desire Too Much of a Good Thing? *Journal of Personality and Social Psychology,* 79, 995-1006.

[7] Vitt, L.A., Danes, S., Hogarth, J., O'Neill, B., Tatom, J., & Walstad, W., Evaluation and Measurement of Learner Outcomes in Financial Education, 2010. http://www.nefe.org /quartercentury

[8] FDIC National Survey of Unbanked and Underbanked Households, 2009. http://www.fdic.gov/householdsurvey/

[9] Council for Economic Education (2009). *A Survey of the States: Economic, Personal Finance & Entrepreneurship Education in Our Nation's Schools in 2009.* http://www.council foreconed.org/about/survey2009/CEE_2009_Survey.pdf

[10] Way, W. and Holden, K. (2009). "Teachers' Background and Capacity to Teach Personal Finance: Results of a National Study." Association for Financial Counseling and Planning Education. http://www.nefe.org/LinkClick.aspx?fileticket=q9Ahp7m5Cbg%3d&tabid=246

[11] Shim, S. and Serido, J. (2011). "Young Adults' Financial Capability: APLUS Arizona Pathways to Life Success for University Students Wave 2." http://www.nefe.org/LinkClick. aspx?fileticket=wDFBV4bfV4E%3d&tabid=711

[12] "Study of Employee Benefits Trends: A Blueprint for the New Benefits Economy," March 2011. MetLife. http://www.metlife.com/assets/institutional/services/insights-and-tools/ebts/EmployeeBenefits-Trends-Study.pdf

[13] Tisdell, E.J., Taylor, E.W. & Sprow, K. (2010). Financial Literacy Education for Adult Learners in Community-Based Programs: Report on the Mixed Method Study of Financial Educators. http://www.nefe.org/LinkClick.aspx?fileticket=CpQ83--pkBA%3d&tabid=1040

[14] Shim, S., Barber, B., Card, N., Xiao & Serido, J. (2009). Financial socialization of young adults: The role of family, work and education. *Journal of Youth and Adolescence*, 39(12), 1457-1470.

[15] Shim, S., Barber, B., Card, N., Xiao & Serido, J. (2009). Financial socialization of young adults: The role of family, work and education. *Journal of Youth and Adolescence*, 39(12), 1457-1470.

[16] Way, W. and Holden, K. (2009). "Teachers' Background and Capacity to Teach Personal Finance: Results of a National Study." Association for Financial Counseling and Planning Education. http://www.nefe.org/LinkClick.aspx?fileticket=q9Ahp7m5Cbg%3d&tabid=246

[17] Hensley, B., Richards, K., & Hansell, W.T. (2012). Responding to the Teacher Training Challenge: Constructing a Research-based Professional Development Model. *Association of Financial Counseling, Planning, Education (AFCPE) 2012 Conference Proceedings*, p. 89-96.
http://6aa7f5c4a9901a3e1a1682793cd11f5a6b732d29.gripelements.com/documents/conferences/2012 _afcpe_proceedings_final.pdf

[18] Shim, S., Barber, B., Card, N., Xiao & Serido, J. (2009). Financial socialization of young adults: The role of family, work and education. *Journal of Youth and Adolescence*, 39(12), 1457-1470.

[19] "Charles Schwab 2008 Parents & Money Survey Findings: Insights into Money Attitudes, Behaviors and Concerns of Parents with Teens." http://www.schwabmoneywise.com /public/file?cmsid=P4054111&cv0

[20] "Fourth Annual Parents, Kids & Money Survey: Detailed Results," (March 2012). T. Rowe Price http://familyeducationmediakit.troweprice.com/wpcontent/uploads/2012/03/T_Rowe_Price_PKM_Survey_Results.pdf

[21] Sledge, J., Tescher, J., & Gordon, S., "From Financial Education to Financial Capability: Opportunities for Innovation," (2010) Center for Financial Services Innovation. http://www.cfsinnovation.com/system/files/Research_Paper_Financial_Capability_Mar2010.pdf

[22] Board of Governors of the Federal Reserve System, "Consumers and Mobile Financial Services." (March 2012). http://www.federalreserve.gov/econresdata/mobiledevice-report-201203.pdf

[23] Federal Register Volume 76, Number 170 (Thursday, September 1, 2011) http://www.gpo.gov/fdsys/pkg/FR-2011-09-01/html/2011-22435.htm

[24] Lusardi, A. and Mitchell, O. (2009) How Ordinary Consumers Make Complex Economic Decisions: Financial Literacy and Retirement Readiness. *National Bureau of Economic Research.*

[25] "Survey: Personal Finance Course Should be a High School Graduation Requirement," Practical Money Skills for LifeTM, (2011). Visa, Inc. http://www.practicalmoneyskills.com/resources/pdfs/Financial_Education_Survey_0411.pdf

[26] Way, W. and Holden, K. (2009). "Teachers' Background and Capacity to Teach Personal Finance: Results of a National Study." Association for Financial Counseling and Planning Education. http://www.nefe.org/LinkClick.aspx?fileticket=q9Ahp7m5Cbg%3d&tabid=246

[27] U.S. Department of Education, National Center for Education Statistics. (2008). *The Condition of Education 2008.* http://nces.ed.gov/pubs2008/2008031.pdf

[28] The Institute for College Access and Success. "Statement on College Board's Trend report." (2009). http://www.ticas.org/files/pub/CB_statement_2009.pdf

[29] Bureau of Labor Statistics, Employment Situation Summary, January 2013. http://www.bls.gov/news.release/empsit.nr0.htm

[30] FINRA Investor Education Foundation, National Survey of the Financial Capability Study, 2009. http://www.finrafoundation/capability

[31] "Stress in America Findings," Stress in America Survey, 2010, page 8. American Psychological Association. http://www.apa.org/news/press/releases/stress/index.aspx

[32] "Study of Employee Benefits Trends: A Blueprint for the New Benefits Economy," March 2011. MetLife. http://www.metlife.com/assets/institutional/services/insights-and-tools/ebts/Employee Benefits-Trends-Study.pdf

[33] Employee Assistance Society of North America Member Survey, December 2008. www.easna.org/wp-content/uploads/2010/08/Release08-12.doc

[34] Shim, S., Barber, B., Card, N., Xiao & Serido, J. (2009). Financial socialization of young adults: The role of family, work and education. *Journal of Youth and Adolescence*, 39(12), 1457-1470.

[35] Holden, K., Kalish, C., Scheinholtz, L., Dietrich, D. & Novak. B. (2009). Financial Literacy Programs Targeted on Pre-School Children: Development and Evaluation. University of Wisconsin-Madison La Follette School Working Paper No. 2009-009. http://www.lafollette.wisc.edu/publications/workingpapers/holden2009-009.pdf

[36] Elliott, W. and Beverly, S. (2011). The role of savings and wealth in reducing "wilt" between expectations and college attendance. *Journal of Children & Poverty*, 17(2), 165-185. First published as CSD Working Paper No. 10-01 (p. 11). http://csd.wustl.edu/Publications/Documents/WP10-01.pdf

[37] Kubisch, A.C., Auspos, P., Brown, P., Chaskin, R., Fulbright-Anderson, K., Hamilton, R., (2002). Voices From the Field II: Reflections on Comprehensive Community Change. Roundtable on Comprehensive Community Initiatives for Children and Families, The Aspen Institute.

[38] U.S. Bureau of Labor Statistics, Employment Situation Summary, January 2013. http://www.bls.gov/news.release/empsit.nr0.htm

Additional Resources Providing Information on Financial Literacy Research:

- "2012 Research Priorities and Research Questions," Financial Literacy and Education Commission (:http://www.treasury.gov/ resource-center/financialeducation/Documents/ 2012%20Research%20Priorities%20-%20May%2012.pdf
- Center for Financial Security, University of Wisconsin-Madison: http://www.cfs.wisc.edu/
- The Federal Reserve Board Economic Research and Data, Board of Governors of the Federal Reserve System: http://www.federalreserve. gov/econresdata/default.htm
- Financial Literacy Center/NEFE Financial Literacy Research Library: http://flresearch.org
- Financial Security Project at Boston College: http://fsp.bc.edu/
- FINRA National Financial Capability Survey: http://usfinancial capability.org
- "From Financial Literacy to Financial Action," McGraw-Hill Research Foundation: http://bit.ly/Financial_Literacy
- Hira, T.K.,"Promoting sustainable financial behavior: implications for education and research," International Journal of Consumer Studies, pp.502-507: http://onlinelibrary.wiley.com/doi/10.1111/j.1470-6431. 2012.01115.x/full
- NEFE Quarter Century Project: http://www.nefe.org/what-we-provide/primary-research/thequarter-century-project-25-years-of-research.aspx
- RAND Financial Literacy Center: www.rand.org/labor/centers/financial-literacy.html

This list of resources is not intended to be exhaustive.

Other Resources Referenced in Report:

Every American Financially Empowered
http://www.whitehouse.gov/sites/default/files/financial_capability_toolkit_5.10.2012.pdf
Money As You Grow
http://www.treasury.gov/resource-center/financial-education/Documents/Money%20as%20You%20Grow.pdf
Financial Capability at Work: A Strategic Framework to Guide Employers http://www.treasury.gov/resource-center/financial-education/Documents/PACFC%20Financial%20Capability%20at%20Work.pdf
Creating Financially Capable Communities: A Resource Guide
http://www.treasury.gov/resource-center/financial-education/Documents/Local%20Guide%20%20Creating%20Financially%20Capable%20Communities.pdf

APPENDIX F: COUNCIL MEMBER BIOGRAPHIES

John W. Rogers, Jr. (Chair)–Chairman, CEO, and Chief Investment Officer, Ariel Investments John W. Rogers, Jr. is the Chairman, CEO, and Chief Investment Officer of Ariel Investments, a firm he founded in 1983 to focus on undervalued small and medium-sized companies. Mr. Rogers currently serves as a board member of Aon Corporation, Exelon Corporation and McDonald's Corporation. Additionally, he is chairman of the Economic Club of Chicago, a director of the Chicago Urban League, a trustee of the University of Chicago, chairman of the board of trustees for the University of Chicago's Laboratory School, and a member of the board of the John S. and James L. Knight Foundation, where he chairs the investment committee. Mr. Rogers served as a co-chair for the 2008 Obama-Biden Presidential Inaugural Committee. In 2008, Mr. Rogers was awarded Princeton University's highest honor, the Woodrow Wilson Award, presented each year to the alumni whose career embodies a commitment to national service. In 2010, he was named an Outstanding Director by the Outstanding Directors Exchange for his leadership on governance, management and diversity in the boardroom.

Amy Rosen (Vice Chair)–President and CEO, the Network for Teaching Entrepreneurship (NFTE) Amy Rosen is President and CEO of the Network for Teaching Entrepreneurship (NFTE), a global nonprofit organization which provides programs designed to inspire young people from low income communities to succeed in school and in life by seizing educational opportunities and starting their own businesses. For over a decade, Rosen has worked on issues confronting the United States public education system as a Fellow at the Broad Urban Superintendents Academy and as the Chief Operating Officer for New Visions for Public Schools. Rosen also served as a Presidential Appointee to the Amtrak Board of Directors, Vice Chairman of the NJ Transit Board of Directors, Deputy Commissioner of the NJ Department of Transportation, and Senior Vice President of Lockheed Martin Information Management Services. Rosen currently Chairs the Board of TEAM SCHOOLS, the network of KIPP Charter Schools in Newark, NJ.

Janie Barrera–Founding President and Chief Executive Officer of ACCION Texas Inc.

Janie Barrera is the founding president and Chief Executive Officer of ACCION Texas Inc. Created in 1994, ACCION Texas Inc. provides small loans and management training to individuals and small businesses in Texas and Louisiana. San Antonio Business Journal listed Ms. Barrera as one of "Twenty Defining Players: People Who Have Helped Shape the City." She also has served on many national, state and local boards, including the Federal Reserve Board's National Consumer Advisory Council. Ms. Barrera received a B.S. from Corpus Christi State University in Corpus Christi, Texas and an M.B.A. from the University of the Incarnate Word in San Antonio, Texas.

Roland Arteaga–President and CEO, Defense Credit Union Council (DCUC)

Roland Arteaga is the President and CEO of the Defense Credit Union Council (DCUC), a position he has held since 2000. In this capacity, he represents the interest of credit unions operating on military bases worldwide, serving as their primary liaison and conduit to the Pentagon. Prior to joining DCUC, Mr. Arteaga served in the United States Army from 1971 to 1999. Among his key assignments while on active duty were his battalion level command of the 230th Finance Support Unit, his deployment to Desert Shield/Desert Storm, his selection as the Senior Military Assistant and Executive Officer to the Assistant Secretary of the Army for Financial Management, and Comptroller and Commander of the United States Army Finance Command at the Pentagon. An ex-officio member of the Defense Credit Union Council's Executive Committee and ex-officio board member and Treasurer of the Armed Forces Financial Network, Arteaga serves on the National Partners Coordinating Committee for the Military Saves campaign and is also a member of the American Society Military Comptrollers.

Ted Beck–President and CEO, National Endowment for Financial Education (NEFE)

Ted Beck is the President and CEO of the National Endowment for Financial Education (NEFE). He is a former member of the President's Advisory Council on Financial Literacy, and currently serves on the FDIC Advisory Committee on Economic Inclusion. He is chairman of the board of the national JumpStart Coalition for Personal Financial Literacy. Prior to his appointment at NEFE, Mr. Beck served as Associate Dean of Executive Education and Corporate Relations at the University of Wisconsin-Madison School of Business, and previously spent more than 20 years in senior management positions for Citibank/Citigroup. Beck currently is an independent trustee of Driehaus Mutual Funds and recently served on the board of the Wisconsin Alumni Association. He previously served as Chairman of the Advisory Board of Directors of Gammex, Inc., and served on the boards of Keylab, Madison Committee on Foreign Relations, International University Consortium for Executive Education, the Graduate School of Banking, the Wisconsin Public Utility Institute, Citicorp Securities, Inc., and the Cleveland Playhouse.

Sherry Salway Black–Director of the Partnership for Tribal Governance, National Congress of American Indians

Sherry Salway Black is the Director of the Partnership for Tribal Governance at the National Congress of American Indians. She is the former Senior Vice President of First Nations Development Institute, a Native-led nonprofit organization that works to improve the economic condition of Native Americans through promoting business development and financial literacy. Ms. Black is a member of the Honoring Nations Board of Governors, a program established by the Harvard Project on American Indian Economic Development to celebrate, document, and disseminate outstanding success stories in governance among American Indian nations. She also serves on the boards of First Peoples Fund and the Johnson Scholarship Foundation. Ms. Black is a member of the Oglala Lakota Nation in Pine Ridge, South Dakota. Ms. Black earned her B.S. from East Stroudsburg University and her M.B.A. from the University of Pennsylvania's Wharton School of Business.

John Hope Bryant–Founder, Chairman and CEO, Operation HOPE

John Hope Bryant is the founder, Chairman and CEO of Operation HOPE, a nonprofit founded in 1992 that focuses on financial literacy and providing financial services for the underbanked in 70 U.S. communities and South Africa. He is also the co-founder of Global Dignity and a member of the Forum of Young Global Leaders for the World Economic Forum and the

Global Agenda Council for the World Economic Forum. Mr. Bryant served as the vice chair of the President's Advisory Council on Financial Literacy (PACFL) and as the chairman of PACFL's Committee on the Underserved. He is also the author of *Love Leadership: The New Way to Lead in a Fear-Based World.* Mr. Bryant has received numerous awards and citations for his work to empower low-wealth communities including the Use Your Life Award from Oprah Winfrey and a 1994 selection by *Time* magazine as one of America's 50 Most Promising Leaders of the Future.

Samuel T. Jackson–Founder, Chairman, and CEO, Economic Empowerment Initiative, Inc.

Samuel T. Jackson is the Founder, Chairman, and CEO of the Economic Empowerment Initiative, Inc., founded in 2001. He is a member of the Board of Directors for the Southern Regional Council, National Association of African-Americans in Human Resources-Atlanta Chapter, Ryan Cameron Foundation, and Georgia Council on Economic Education. Mr. Jackson was honored with the Martin Luther King, Jr. Community Service Award by Emory University's Goizueta Business School and Rollins School of Public Health for excellence in community innovation and change.

Richard Ketchum–Chairman and CEO, Financial Industry Regulatory Authority (FINRA)

Richard Ketchum is the Chairman and CEO of the Financial Industry Regulatory Authority (FINRA). Prior to joining FINRA, he was CEO of NYSE Regulation, Chief Regulatory Officer of the New York Stock Exchange and General Counsel of the Corporate and Investment Bank of Citigroup, Inc. Previously, he spent 12 years at the National Association of Securities Dealers and the NASDAQ Stock Market, Inc., where he served as president of both organizations. He also worked at the Securities and Exchange Commission for 14 years, with eight of those years as Director of the Division of Market Regulation. He currently sits on the Board of Directors of Appleseed, a non-profit network of 16 public interest justice centers in the United States and Mexico.

Beth Kobliner–Personal Finance Commentator, Journalist, and Author

Beth Kobliner is a personal finance commentator, journalist, and author of the *New York*

Times bestseller *Get a Financial Life: Personal Finance in Your Twenties and Thirties*. She has written on a broad range of personal finance topics for publications including *Money* magazine, *The New York Times*, *Reader's Digest*, and *Glamour,* and she has regular columns on *The Huffington Post*,

Mint.com, and in *Redbook* magazine. She has been a frequent commentator on NBC's *Today* show, ABC's *Good Morning America*, CBS's *Early Show*, and the national public radio shows *The Takeaway* and *Marketplace*. Ms. Kobliner served as a content advisor and on-air financial expert to Elmo for Sesame Workshop's first-ever financial education initiative, a bilingual outreach program. She is a regular lecturer on financial literacy for children of all ages at schools including the Children's Storefront in Harlem, the New Jersey Institute of Technology, and Yale University.

Marc H. Morial-- President and CEO of the National Urban League

Marc H. Morial is President and CEO of the National Urban League. Mr. Morial served as Mayor of New Orleans, Louisiana from 1994 until 2002. During that time, he was President of the U.S. Conference of Mayors. From 1992 to 1994, he served in the Louisiana State Senate. Earlier in his career, Mr. Morial practiced law from 1985 until 1994 and was an adjunct law professor at Xavier University of Louisiana from 1986 to 1990. Mr. Morial has a B.A. in Economics from the University of Pennsylvania and a J.D. from Georgetown University.

Addison Barry Rand–CEO, AARP

Addison Barry Rand is Chief Executive Officer of AARP, a nonprofit, nonpartisan organization with a membership that helps people 50+ have independence, choices and control in ways that are beneficial and affordable to them and society as a whole. He has served as Chairman and Chief Executive Officer of Avis Group Holdings, Chief Executive Officer of Equitant Ltd., and Executive Vice President for Worldwide Operations at Xerox Corporation. Mr. Rand has served as the Chairman of the Board of Trustees at Howard University since 2006 and has also served on the boards of the Urban Family Institute, the Congressional Black Caucus Foundation and the Garth Fagan Dance Theatre. In 1993 he was inducted into the National Sales and Marketing Hall of Fame and is a recipient of the NAACP Image Award.

Carrie Schwab-Pomerantz–President, Charles Schwab Foundation

Carrie Schwab-Pomerantz is president of the Charles Schwab Foundation, a private, nonprofit organization funded by The Charles Schwab Corporation, whose mission is to create positive change through financial education, philanthropy, and volunteerism. Schwab-Pomerantz writes extensively about personal finance; her work includes a weekly educational column distributed through schwab.com and Creators News Service as well as a book on family finance entitled *It Pays to Talk: How to Have the Essential Conversations with your Family about Money and Investing*. In her efforts to advance financial literacy, Schwab-Pomerantz has spearheaded several programs, including

Money Matters: Make It Count, a national program for teens, created in collaboration with the Boys & Girls Clubs of America.

Eldar Shafir -- William Stewart Tod Professor of Psychology and Public Affairs, Department of Psychology and Woodrow Wilson School for Public and International Affairs, Princeton University

Eldar Shafir is the William Stewart Tod Professor of Psychology and Public Affairs in the Department of Psychology and the Woodrow Wilson School for Public and International Affairs at Princeton University. Dr. Shafir's research focuses on descriptive analyses of decision making, and on issues related to behavioral economics, with a focus on decision making in the context of poverty and on the application of behavioral research to policy. He is Past President of the Society for Judgment and Decision Making, a member of the Russell Sage Foundation Behavioral Economics Roundtable, Research Affiliate of Innovations for Poverty Action, and Fellow of the Filene Research Institute, the Canadian Institute for Advanced Research, and the Institute for Quantitative Social Science at Harvard University. He is cofounder and director of Ideas42, a social science research and development lab. Dr. Shafir received his B.A. from Brown University and a Ph.D. in Cognitive Science from MIT.

Kenneth Wade–Senior Community Affairs Executive of Global Marketing & Corporate Affairs, Bank of America

Kenneth Wade is a Senior Community Affairs Executive of Global Marketing & Corporate Affairs for Bank of America; in that role he is responsible for enhancing the bank's relationships with key organizations in consumer affairs and community development. Mr. Wade joined Bank of America on January 1, 2011. Prior to his role at Bank of America, Mr. Wade was CEO for NeighborWorks America, a national non-profit organization that provides training, technical and financial assistance to more than 3,000 community development nonprofits throughout the U.S. focused on affordable housing, foreclosure mitigation and neighborhood stabilization initiatives. Mr. Wade has more than 35 years of experience in community development in a variety of organizations.

In: Federal Recommendations
Editor: Crystal M. Kirby
ISBN: 978-1-63117-038-6

Chapter 2

FINANCIAL CAPABILITY AT WORK: A STRATEGIC FRAMEWORK FOR EMPLOYERS*

President's Advisory Council on Financial Capability, Partnerships Committee

OVERVIEW

Background

The President's Advisory Council on Financial Capability (PACFC) believes that the workplace offers a critically important and trusted delivery point for financial education and related benefits, with the potential to positively impact as many as 138 million Americans.

---

* This is an edited, reformatted and augmented version of a President's Advisory Council on Financial Capability, Partnerships Committee publication, dated September 4, 2012.

Business Rationale

Increasingly, employers of all sizes are concluding that in order to be competitive, enhance productivity and drive employee retention, they want and need to provide financial education, benefits and resources that go beyond just saving for retirement.

- 76% of Americans say they are stressed about money.[1]
- 58% of employers say financial stress contributes to employee absences.[2]
- 78% of employers say employees are less productive at work when they are worried about personal financial issues. [2]
- Retirement experts generally recommend that individuals need between 70% and 80% of pre-retirement income – from a combination of sources including Social Security benefits, pensions, and personal savings – to achieve income adequacy in retirement.

The Challenge

The PACFC recommends that our nation's employers serve as leaders and role models by providing the five fundamentals – and working toward offering advanced features – to drive financial capability among America's workers.

Sources: [1] American Psychological Association Survey, 2010; [2] MetLife Study on Employee Benefits Trends, 2010.

CHALLENGING EVERY EMPLOYER TO MAKE A DIFFERENCE

Getting the five fundamentals in place to help employees improve their financial outcomes

		Micro / Small Employers	Mid / Large Employers	Advanced Features
1	Benefits	Provide access to a retirement savings vehicle such as a SEP IRA, payroll deduction IRA, or SIMPLE IRA, preferably with an employer contribution and/or match. Also consider providing a defined benefit (e.g. multi-employer plan), profit sharing or low-cost defined contribution plan with the features recommended for Mid/Large Employers (at right).	Provide a defined benefit, profit sharing, or low-cost 401(k), 403(b), 457 defined contribution plan with the following features: -Auto-enrollment -Employer contributions -Default auto-investment in professionally managed / appropriate asset allocation (such as target-date fund, broad-based index ETF, etc.)	Enhanced defined contribution saving / investing features such as: - Auto-escalation of annual deferrals - Employer contribution regardless of employee participation - Auto-enrollment for all employees (not just new hires) - Low-cost annuity investment option Supplementary defined benefit/contribution plan Investment guidance Financial assessment and one-on-one counseling
2	Educational resources	Provide opportunities for employees to learn from an objective source the core competencies of money management: - Budgeting - Saving / Goal-setting - Borrowing / Debt management - Insurance / Income protection - Retirement planning / Investing	Provide opportunities for employees to learn from an objective source the core competencies of money management: - Budgeting - Saving / Goal-setting - Borrowing / Debt management - Insurance / Income protection - Retirement planning / Investing	Additional educational topics to cover: - Buying a home - Saving for college - Getting ready to retire - Long-term care Online tools and calculators
3	Marketing	Actively encourage employees to take advantage of the education and benefits. Employers should serve as visible champions of the efforts.	Create campaigns and communications that actively encourage employees to take advantage of the education and benefits. CEO / C-Suite leadership should serve as visible champions of the efforts.	- Multi-channel delivery (live, online) - Trigger-based messages (at birthdays, employment anniversaries, birth, etc) - Family inclusion, testimonials and peer-to-peer sharing - Manager engagement plan - Leverage employee diversity/resource groups
4	Measurement and metrics	Set specific, measurable goals and track progress. Key metrics include retirement savings plan participation and education participation.	Set specific, measurable goals and track progress at least annually. Key metrics include: 401(k) enrollment, deferral, diversification, balances and loans; educational participation; marketing results.	- Quarterly results summary / report - Segmented analysis by employee demographic - Dedicated staff and budget to implement program and track results
5	Products and services	Facilitate employee relationship with a bank or credit union by providing direct deposit.	Facilitate employee relationship with a bank or credit union by providing: - Direct deposit - Prescreened providers	- Negotiated preferred pricing / services - Enable direct deposit into multiple accounts, such as savings, 529, etc.

RESOURCES FOR EMPLOYERS*

AARP / FINRA / Retirement Security Project's Retirement Made Simpler	A coalition formed by AARP, the Financial Industry Regulatory Authority (FINRA) and the Retirement Security Project to provide companies with the tools, research and resources to make informed decisions about automating their retirement plans. Retirementmadesimpler.org
American Savings and Education Council / Employee Benefit Research Institute	ASEC is a nonprofit coalition of public and private organizations whose goal is to make saving and retirement planning a priority for all Americans. www.asec.org EBRI supports the development of sound employee benefits programs and public policy. www.ebri.org
Money Smart / Money Smart for Small Business	Created by the Federal Deposit Insurance Corporation (FDIC), Money Smart is a curriculum to help low- and moderate-income individuals improve their financial skills. They have also created a version of the program for small-business owners. fdic.gov/moneysmart
MyMoney.gov	MyMoney.gov is the federal government website featuring federal financial literacy and education programs, grants, and other consumer information, including information on Earned Income Tax Credit, health insurance and more. It is available in Spanish and English. www.mymoney.gov
National Endowment for Financial Education	- Resources on how to plan and deliver financial workshops: financialworkshopkits.org - Free beginner's guide to financial readiness: smartaboutmoney.org - Retirement resources for employees: myretirementpaycheck.org
NYSE / Financial Literacy Center Workplace Financial Fitness Kit	Online resources for employers and employees: nyse.nyx.com/financial-fitness-kit
Small Business Retirement Savings Advisor	Developed by the Department of Labor and Employee Benefits Security Administration, the Small Business Retirement Savings Advisor provides guidance about retirement savings options for small businesses. dol.gov/ebsa/publications/SEPPlans.html
Workplace Leaders in Financial Education Awards	Sponsored by Society for Human Resources Management and AICPA, the Workplace Leaders in Financial Education Award recognizes companies and institutions for exemplary financial literacy efforts: wlife.org/
World at Work	A nonprofit organization providing education, conferences and research focused on global human resources issues including compensation, benefits, work-life and integrated total rewards to attract, motivate and retain a talented workforce: worldatwork.org

* This list of objective, conflict-free resources is for reference only. It is not intended to be exhaustive. It does not endorse or promote specific initiatives, research, or organizations.

SUPPORTING RESEARCH*

401(k) Plans in Living Color: A Study of 401(k) Disparities Across Racial and Ethnic Groups	Headline: Study reveals retirement plans of African-Americans and Hispanics hit especially hard during tough economy: arielinvestments.com/401k-Study-2012/ Survey Sponsor: Ariel Investments and AON Hewitt. (April, 2012)
Help in Defined Contribution Plans: 2006 through 2010	Headline: 401(k) participants using professional investment help continue to do better than those who go it alone: aon.mediaroom.com/index.php?s=43&item=2388 Survey Sponsor: AON Hewitt and Financial Engines. (September, 2011)
The New Rules of Engagement for 401(k) Plans: Shifting Focus to Outcomes that Matter	Headline: Professional advice has a direct and positive impact on the behavior of 401(k) plan participants. www.aboutschwab.com/press/research/retirement_research/ Survey Sponsor: Charles Schwab, a 401(k) service provider to approximately 1.5 million company retirement plan participants. (September, 2010)
9th Annual Study of Employment Benefits Trends / Section 04: Remodeling the Benefits and Retirement Space	This broad-based survey on employee benefits contained several findings related to employees' financial health, including that employees with stressful financial situations report poorer health, and financial stress contributes to absenteeism and stifles on-the-job productivity. www.metlife.com/business/insights-and-tools/industry-knowledge/employee-benefits-trends-study/index.html#highlights Survey Sponsors: MetLife (March, 2011)
Financial Education: An Essential Component of Your Wellness Strategy	Headline: By offering broad-based financial advice and guidance, employers can help employees achieve their financial objectives and an overall sense of financial wellness. In turn, employers can profit from a more productive workforce and increase the appreciation of the benefits they provide. www.metlife.com/assets/institutional/services/insights-and-tools/cwb/ml-plansmart-whitepaper.pdf Survey Sponsor: MetLife (June, 2011)
Increasing the Effectiveness of Retirement Saving Programs for Females and Low Income Employees: A Marketing Approach	Headline: Effective employee communications programs can measurably reduce employee anxiety about retirement financial needs, and increase participation in and contributions to supplementary retirement accounts, compared to a control group. www.nefe.org/LinkClick.aspx?fileticket=HqSDPBWhVZk=&tabid=758 Authors: Annamaria Lusardi, Punam Keller, Adam Keller. Survey Sponsors: National Endowment for Financial Education, Dartmouth (April, 2009)

* This list of resources is for reference only. It is not intended to be exhaustive. It does not endorse or promote specific initiatives, research, or organizations.

In: Federal Recommendations
Editor: Crystal M. Kirby

ISBN: 978-1-63117-038-6

Chapter 3

CREATING FINANCIALLY CAPABLE COMMUNITIES: A RESOURCE GUIDE*

President's Advisory Council on Financial Capability

BACKGROUND

The President's Advisory Council on Financial Capability (PACFC) was created by Executive Order 13530, signed by President Barack Obama on January 29, 2010. Its charter is to advise the President on promoting and enhancing financial literacy and capability among the American people.

While the PACFC cannot by federal statute become operational, it is charged with providing financial capability policy recommendations for the nation to the President of the United States. The Partnerships Subcommittee and the Subcommittee on the Underserved and Community Empowerment encourage public- and private-sector collaboration to strengthen the financial capability of Americans in communities throughout the country.

One priority of the PACFC is to encourage the creation of state, tribal and local financial capability initiatives to build financial security for individuals and economic well-being for their communities at large.

* This is an edited, reformatted and augmented version of President's Advisory Council on Financial Capability publication, dated March 2012.

What Is Financial Capability?

Executive Order 13530, which established the PACFC, defines financial capability as the capacity, based on knowledge, skills and access, to manage financial resources effectively.

The Purpose of This Document

The goal of this document is to inspire local leaders to leverage partnerships to create their own financial capability initiatives as a means toward building financial well-being in their communities – a prerequisite for competing and winning in a global economy.

This document serves as a resource guide and a roadmap to help regional, state, tribal and local leaders get started with their own financial capability initiatives. While it provides many specific examples of impactful work happening around the country, this document is intended for reference only, and is not intended to endorse or promote specific initiatives.

Why State, Tribal and Local Leadership Matters

Local leaders in states, tribes, local governments and communities play a critical role in helping people improve their financial capability. Because local leaders have a unique understanding of the economic, financial and educational obstacles that negatively impact the people in their communities, they are in a strong position to drive local strategies and initiatives that can make a real difference.

Many states, tribes and local governments are already leading the charge and have made significant and measurable impact. Some examples include, but are certainly not limited to, the states of Delaware and Wisconsin; the cities of San Francisco, Miami, New York, and Savannah, Georgia; and American Indian Tribes such as Citizen Potawatomi Nation in Oklahoma and Eastern Band of Cherokee Indians in North Carolina, among others.

Successful states, tribes and localities leverage existing resources and infrastructure – and they utilize partnerships across the public, private and nonprofit sectors – to implement innovative programs that improve the financial well-being and outcomes of their citizens. They have clear objectives, well-defined program implementation and marketing strategies, and outcomes-driven metrics. Successful jurisdictions also share their findings, best-practices, and challenges with other communities.

The PACFC has identified three broad areas for financial capability initiatives:

- Financial education and capability programs for youth,
- Financial capability and access for low- to moderate-income families and the underserved,
- Financial capability in the workplace.

This document is organized to help communities address these critical areas.

KEY STEPS TO CREATING LOCAL FINANCIAL CAPABILITY INITIATIVES

Step 1: Evaluate the Local Landscape, and Make a Case for Addressing Financial Capability

To build local support and develop working partnerships to advance financial capability in communities, stakeholders need to understand why financial capability is an important issue, what's currently being done in the community to address the issue, what's at stake in communities with poor financial health, and how strong financial behaviors and outcomes among community members can have a positive impact on a community's overall economic health.

It's important to begin by evaluating the current landscape. Conduct an inventory of organizations and programs that are already involved with or are addressing financial empowerment initiatives, such as financial literacy and education, asset-building, financial coaching, tax-preparation assistance, and anything else related to financial capability. Keep in mind that many banks and foundations fund this type of work at the local level, so it may make sense to find out which initiatives have been successful, and include representatives from those initiatives in the discussion.

Key elements of a business case could include:

A. Your state's performance on the FINRA Investor Education Foundation's National Financial Capability Study, where you'll find how your state compares to other states and the nation as a whole on five measures: spending vs. saving, emergency savings, non-bank borrowing, financial literacy, and comparison shopping: usfinancialcapability.org
B. Your state's performance on the CFED (Corporation for Enterprise Development) Assets & Opportunity Scorecard, a state-by-state performance and policy analysis on five areas: Financial Assets & Income, Businesses & Jobs, Housing & Homeownership, Health Care and Education: cfed.org/scorecard
C. Local rates of "unbanked"/"underbanked" individuals Research your community at webtools.joinbankon.org/community/search
D. Local foreclosure rates. Websites such as realtytrac.com can provide statistics.
E. Local performance on financial capability among the general population and/ or specific segments such as youth and workers. Local/state insights may be culled from national studies and resources, including:
   i. Employee Benefit Research Institute: ebri.org
   ii. Gallup Hope Index: www.operationhope.org/page/pgid/39
   iii. Jump$tart Coalition for Personal Financial Literacy: jumpstart.org
   iv. State-by-state results on the National Financial Capability Challenge: challenge.treas.gov
F. Information and testimonials about how other communities have embraced financial capability and improved the financial well-being of their citizens. Some examples include Delaware, Wisconsin, New York City, San Francisco, Indianapolis, San Antonio, Seattle-King County, Savannah, Providence, American Indian and Alaska Native Tribes, and many others. (See Resource Guide/Appendix.)

Step 2: Create a Local Council

A local financial literacy/financial capability council is a formalized group of influential individuals representing governments, education leaders, nonprofit organizations, academia, private foundations, and private industry who agree to serve voluntarily with the collective goal of enhancing financial literacy and capability among the state, tribe or local community.

Potential Benefits of Creating a Local Council

- **Builds efficiency** by sharing information and resources across multiple organizations with similar goals.
- **Encourages innovation** by bringing unique points of view and areas of expertise to the table.
- **Helps communities set strategic priorities** through collaboration and cross-institutional partnership.
- **Maximizes resources by pooling human and financial capital** to jointly solve problems and minimize duplicative programs in local areas.
- **Creates greater visibility and cross-community support** by helping to ensure that resources are focused where the impact can be greatest.

Who Should Lead and Be Part of a Council?

Councils can take many shapes and sizes. In fact, it's critical that they be customized to the unique needs and circumstances of the local community. Members of the PACFC held meetings and learning sessions with state and city councils and leaders to identify common practices that lead to successful local efforts. Through those discussions, several common themes and recommendations emerged.

By and large, experts agree that councils can be most effective when they include influential leaders and decision-makers, such as the following:

- Government leaders, both elected and high-level career staff, who can prioritize public resources and leverage a "bully pulpit" to improve visibility and awareness of the issues and solutions.
- Education leaders, including school superintendents, who can effect change within the existing education infrastructure and among local youth.
- Financial education experts, including nonprofit and community-based organizations, professional associations, Cooperative Extension services and others with expertise in delivering financial education and capability content. Examples include the Financial Planning Association (FPA), the National Association of Personal Financial Advisors (NAPFA) and the Association for Financial Counseling, Planning and Education (AFCPE).
- Nonprofit organizations, libraries, and other community service providers with expertise serving specific populations such as youth, underserved individuals and low- to moderate-income families.

- Academics and researchers, who bring extensive knowledge, data, and objective analysis of what works and what does not.
- Local business leaders, particularly those from financial institutions such as banks and credit unions, who bring business and financial acumen, product- development expertise, and financial and professional (pro bono) resources.
- Local community members who may be struggling with financial instability themselves, or who may offer practical insights on the issues and concerns of community members.
- Other stakeholders who can share unique perspectives, such as youth leaders, retirees, and other engaged residents.

For a step-by-step guide to getting a Financial Literacy Council off the ground in your community, see "**Steps for Launching a Local Financial Literacy/Financial Capability Council**," in the appendix.

Step 3: Focus the Work

Determine key areas of focus for the jurisdiction's financial capability work and then establish committees or working teams to be responsible for each area of focus. Each jurisdiction will have unique priorities. However, the PACFC recommends three broad areas that will be relevant to any community:

1) Youth financial education and capability,
2) Financial access for the underserved,
3) Financial capability through the workplace.

Step 4: Articulate Clear Goals and Metrics

Create a core list of financial literacy and financial capability goals and objectives that will drive positive outcomes and enhance the lives of community members.

Following is a sample, noncomprehensive list of example goals and metrics:

- Every public high-school student in [jurisdiction] will participate in the National Financial Capability Challenge beginning in 20XX.

- Every public school student in [jurisdiction] will complete financial capability education upon graduation, beginning with the class of 20XX.
- 50% of all employers in [jurisdiction] will voluntarily implement financial education that aligns with U.S. Treasury Department's Core Competencies by 20XX.
- [Jurisdiction] will reduce the rate of unbanked individuals by 60% over 5 years.
- [Jurisdiction] will reduce the foreclosure rate by 40% within the next 18 months.

Step 5: Develop and Launch Programs That Address the Stated Goals

Consider adopting some of the following programs and initiatives, many of which have been successfully implemented in other jurisdictions. The initiatives are organized under the PACFC's three core areas of focus: financial education for youth, financial capability and access for the underserved, and financial capability in the workplace.

Financial Education for Youth

1) Encourage and/or incentivize your school district to develop a K-12 plan to fully integrate curriculum that is aligned with what young people need to know, at what ages, in order to become financially capable. Developing strategies to align this work with goals established by the Common Core – and integrating appropriate teacher training – should be included. At the same time, encourage outside learning with organizations like Junior Achievement, Boys & Girls Clubs of America, Lemonade Day, and Savings Plans with Incentives.

Resources to support these plans, as well as information concerning state mandates and local resources, can be found at jumpstart.org and councilforeconed.org. "Money Milestones'" is another useful resource and can be accessed at moneyasyougrow.org.

2) Establish programs in public schools to ensure all students have the knowledge necessary to undertake financial planning for college and career goals, including:
    - Financial management for working youth,

- Ensuring students understand the connection between education and potential income,
- Ensuring college-bound students understand the FAFSA form, reduce their exposure to higher interest private loans, and maximize their capture of federal loans.

The U.S. Department of Education FAFSA website provides resources at fafsa.ed.gov/. John Hancock High School in Chicago is an example of the impact of such programs. Counselors at the school helped students access about $3.5 million in grants and financial aid last year, up from $5,000 just a few years earlier. The school's college enrollment rate has also increased from 49 percent in 2008 to 80 percent in 2010.

3) Encourage and/or incentivize local high schools to participate in the National Financial Capability Challenge, which raises awareness about the need for financial capability efforts and is sponsored by the U.S. Department of Treasury and recommended by the PACFC. Participating students and schools are eligible for scholarships and grants.
    - Learn more about the National Financial Capability Challenge at challenge.treas.gov
4) Ensure that youth summer jobs provided by the state, tribe or local government incorporate direct deposit, savings accounts, and financial capability and financial literacy training.
    - The Economics Awareness Council in Chicago implemented such an initiative. Learn more at econcouncil.org.
5) Encourage local youth-services organizations to adopt programs that deliver financial education. Examples include:
    - Boys & Girls Clubs of America's Money Matters: Make It Count: moneymattersmakeitcount.com
    - Junior Achievement: ja.org
    - Boys Scouts and Girls Scouts personal finance badges: scouting.org, girlscouts.org

Financial Capability Access for the Underserved

1) Conduct an assessment of your community's needs and identify local barriers to financial stability for residents. Consider evaluating the number of unbanked individuals, as well as whether and why individuals are using "alternative" banking services such as pay-day lenders and check-cashing services. This information will help inform

the types of programs, products and services that may be needed in your community.

2) Set targets for improving financial capability in your community – and focus on addressing the needs and/or problems you identified in your assessment/ evaluation. For example, if your goal is to reduce the number of unbanked individuals in your community, set a realistic target for how many people you would like to impact. Many communities have successfully leveraged BankOn and similar programs to achieve their targets. These programs are partnerships typically between banks/credit unions, community partners and government entities to provide access to low-cost, safe accounts and financial education for unbanked, usually low-income individuals.
   - The website joinbankon.org provides state, tribal and local data on the un- and under-banked and many resources on starting a Bank On initiative, as well as the ability to participate in discussions with other Bank On leaders.
3) Establish an awareness campaign and/or website to keep the local conversation growing and to provide tools to parents, families, and self-employed and micro business owners. For examples, see these websites:
   - indyscampaign.org
   - standbymede.org
4) Utilize business education and economic programs for self employed and local minority small businesses to help them manage their finances and grow their wealth. Programming could include:
   - U.S. Small Business Administration and SBA Direct: sba.gov
   - Startup America: www.s.co
   - Association for Enterprise Opportunity: microenterpriseworks.org
   - Kauffman Foundation: Kauffman.org
5) Support an area-wide (state, tribe, city) Earned Income Tax Credit (EITC) campaign to help low-income workers learn how to access their benefits.
   - Corporate Voices for Working Families offers free employer guides and EITC educational and marketing toolkits at www.corporatevoices.org.
   - Some examples from cities that have implemented EITC programs:
     i. Los Angeles: greaterlaeitc.org

ii. Washington, D.C.: dceitc.org

6) Support initiatives to provide financial education at teachable moments. For example, some cities are incorporating FAFSA help with tax assistance provided at IRS offices for national VITA (Voluntary Income Tax Assistance) coalitions.
    - Ladder Up is an organization that demonstrates how this can work in practice: goladderup.org.

Financial Capability in the Workplace

1) Hold meetings and/or summits with state, tribal and local employers and encourage the adoption of employee benefits that align with the PACFC private industry recommendations.
2) Draft a formal recommendation that your state, tribal or local government adopt employee benefits/workplace financial capability programs for its own employees that align with the PACFC's "Proposed Recommendation Regarding Financial Capability Resources for Federal Employees," available here: http://www.treasury.gov/resource-center/financial-education/Documents/FINAL%20Federal%20Employee%20Recommendation%201-19-12.pdf
3) Encourage local employers to compete in the Workplace Leaders in Financial Education Awards, sponsored by the American Institute of Certified Public Accountants (AICPA) and the Society for Human Resources Management (SHRM). Learn more at wlife.org.
4) Encourage self-employed, micro- and small-business owners to utilize CDFI and credit unions to minimize banking fees, build their savings, and separate their personal and business transactions.

Other initiatives

The following ideas and initiatives may support more than one of the core areas of focus listed above (youth, access for the underserved, and workplace):

1. Create Financial Education Networks, whereby local nonprofits, educators, practitioners, librarians, government leaders and others get to know each others' areas of expertise and programming, and find opportunities to share best practices and maximize local resources. San Francisco and New York City provide Financial Education Network information and resources:

- San Francisco: frbsf.org/community/issues/fensf.html
- New York City: nyc.gov/html/ofe/html/providers/join.shtml

1) Be inclusive and further encourage partnerships by hosting financial literacy town hall meetings, roundtables, conferences, and listening sessions to share ideas, collaborate, and explore new ways to enhance local financial capability.
2) See an example of a press release announcing a listening session in Indianapolis at www.bankonindy.org first-lady-of-indianapolis-to-host-listening-session-with- u-s-treasury-official-and-members-of-presidents-advisory-council-on-financial- capability/
3) Create a local "financial literacy corps" that provides a centralized local resource for information on financial literacy volunteer opportunities across the state/tribe/city.
4) Build interest in your work by leveraging existing public awareness campaigns, such as:
   - National Financial Literacy Month: whitehouse.gov/the-press-office/2011/03/31/ presidential-proclamation-national-financial-literacy-month
   - Money Smart Week: chicagofed.org/webpages/education/msw/index.cfm
   - America Saves Week: americasaves.org

Step 6: Measure Your Impact and Adjust Your Programs Accordingly

As with any successful initiative, it's critical to establish at the outset clear objectives, as well as clear milestones, benchmarks and metrics for measuring success. (See Step 4.) Consider whether the chosen goals are implementable and achievable, given economic realities and conflicting pressures for time and money.

If initiatives fall short of achieving the established goals, carefully evaluate which factors or elements of the program to adjust. Reconsider whether the goals themselves are realistic for your community. And regardless of whether you're meeting all your goals, be sure to share your findings and results with other jurisdictions so they can learn from your experience.

- National Endowment for Financial Education's research-based customizable Evaluation Toolkit offers methods to measure program impact. The toolkit is available here: http://toolkit.nefe.org

RESOURCE GUIDE

This list of resources is not intended to be exhaustive.

Organization	Resource Details	Contact/Info
Cities for Financial Empowerment Coalition	Cities for Financial Empowerment (CFE) brings together pioneering municipal governments from across the country that have begun to use their power and positions to advance innovative financial empowerment initiatives.	cfecoalition.org
Corporation for Enterprise Development	CFED programs test and refine promising ideas to find out what works. Programs include matching funds, IDAs, asset-building for children, self-employment tax initiative.	cfed.org
	In addition, the CFED Scorecard reviews state-by-state performance and policy measures across five areas: Financial Assets & Income; Business & Jobs; Housing & Homeownership; Healthcare and Education.	cfed.org/scorecard
Council for Economic Education	CEE offers comprehensive K-12 economic and personal finance education programs, including the basics of entrepreneurship, consisting of teaching resources across the curriculum, professional development for teachers, and nationally-normed assessment instruments.	councilforeconed.org
Delaware's Stand by Me program	The Delaware Financial Empowerment Partnership (DFEP) is a joint venture of the State of Delaware and the United Way of Delaware, providing a package of financial empowerment services called $tand By Me.	standbymede.org
Financial Education Network of San Francisco	The Financial Education Network – San Francisco (FEN-SF) is a collaborative group of San Francisco's nonprofit service providers, philanthropic funders, and local public sector representatives dedicated to improving financial education services in the City.	frbsf.org/community /issues/ fensf.html

Organization	Resource Details	Contact/Info
Financial Literacy Center/ New York Stock Exchange Foundation	NYSE Foundation and the Financial Literacy Center provide free resources for employers and employees.	nyse.nyx.com/financial-fitness-kit
Financial Literacy and Education Commission	Free, unbiased resources from more than 20 federal agencies on array of financial topics.	mymoney.gov
First Nations Development Institute	Provides financial education training to Native communities and tribal governments.	www.firstnations.org
Gallup Hope Index	Measures financial literacy in relationship to hope, wellbeing, and engagement among U.S. students in grades 5 through 12.	www.operationhope.org/ page/pgid/39
Indianapolis Campaign for Financial Fitness	ICFF is a coalition of public and private organizations that helps Indianapolis residents and their families manage their finances. The goal is to achieve the improved quality of life that accompanies financial stability at any income level.	indyscampaign.org
Join Bank On	Research your community's under- and un-banked stats, and learn how to start a Bank On program in your area.	JoinBankOn.org
Jump$tart Coalition for Personal Finance	Jump$tart is a national coalition of organizations dedicated to improving the financial literacy of pre-kindergarten through college-age youth by providing advocacy, research, standards and educational resources.	jumpstart.org
Money Milestones	Money Milestones are the 20 essential financial lessons that kids need to know as they grow. They're written in easy-to-understand language, aimed at parents and children, and organized into 4 key concepts per age group.	moneyasyougrow.org
National Congress of American Indians	Works with tribal leaders on training and technical assistance on significant issue areas including financial education. Also conducts a Tribal Exchange on the Stock Market.	ncai.org
National Endowment for Financial Education – consumer and educator resources	NEFE offers consumer resources, an interactive video sharing site, a high-school financial planning program, and a site dedicated to community financial education instructors.	smartaboutmoney.org spendster.org hsfpp.nefe.org www.financialworkshop kits.org

(Continued)

Organization	Resource Details	Contact/Info
National Endowment for Financial Education – Resources for employers	NEFE provides employers with a research-based step-by-step process to increase retirement savings plan participation, particularly among low-income and female employees.	retirementtlc.org
National Financial Capability Challenge	Information about the National Financial Capability Challenge, a financial capability test for high-school students sponsored by the U.S. Department of Treasury.	challenge.treas.gov
National Financial Capability Study	The FINRA Investor Education Foundation commissioned this national study of the financial capability of American adults. The overarching research objectives were to benchmark key indicators of financial capability and evaluate how these indicators vary with underlying demographic, behavioral, attitudinal and financial literacy characteristics.	finrafoundation.org/capability usfinancialcapability.org
National League of Cities	NLC Bank On Toolkit for Municipalities Banking on Opportunity: A Scan of the Evolving Field of Bank On Initiatives.	nlc.org/find-city-solutions/ iyef/family-economic-success/ asset-building/bank-on-cities-toolkit www.treasury.gov/ resource-center/financial-education/Documents/ Banking%20On%20Opportunity %20Nov% 2011.pdf
Native CDFI Network	Coalition of more than 69 members to help strengthen the Native Community Development Financial Institution industry through which a significant amount of financial education for Native communities takes place.	facebook.com/Native-CDFI- Network

Organization	Resource Details	Contact/Info
SHRM and AICPA's Workplace Leaders in Financial Education Awards	Awards program that recognizes organizations with exemplary workplace financial literacy efforts to enhance employee financial well-being and encourages employers to implement and further develop financial literacy programs.	Wlife.org
United Way	In 2008, United Way initiated an ambitious 10-year plan to cut in half the number of lower-income families who are financially unstable. This site provides information about how local United Way organizations are helping drive financial stability in their communities.	unitedway.org/our-work/ income
Wisconsin Governor's Council on Financial Literacy	Link to Council webpage, with mission and initiatives. Link to the Executive Order establishing the Council.	wdfi.org/ymm/govcouncilf inlit wdfi.org/_resources/ indexed/ site/ymm/govcouncilfinlit/ ExecOrder24.pdf

APPENDIX

Steps for Launching a Local Financial Literacy/ Financial Capability Council

1. Identify a leader for the Council

Identify a leader or official within the jurisdiction who has the mandate, influence, and stature in the government and community to lead the Council effort. (For example, in San Francisco the effort is led by the City Treasurer; in New York City, the effort is led by the Commissioner of the Department of Consumer Affairs.)

2. Recruit Council members

Identify influential government officials and/or elected officials, representatives of businesses (both financial and non-financial), non-profit organizations, academic institutions, private foundations and other individuals who are willing and eager to engage on the topic financial literacy, capability, and empowerment.

3. Take official steps to create the Council

This could mean encouraging legislation to create the Council or encourage state, county or city executive branch leaders to create it by executive order. See examples of executive orders in the Resource Guide.

4. Formally kick off the Council

Host a preliminary hearing and/or meeting in your area around the "State of Financial Literacy and Financial Capability." Announce the establishment of the Council and its charter.

5. Focus the work

Choose two or three key areas of focus for the Council's initial energy. Form subcommittees in each of these areas. For example, the President's Advisory Council on Financial Capability is focusing on three key areas: 1) Youth financial education and capability; 2) Financial access for the underserved; 3) Financial capability through the workplace.

6. Articulate clear goals and metrics

Create a core list of financial literacy and financial capability goals and objectives that will enhance the lives of community members.

Examples: Every public school student in [jurisdiction] will complete financial capability education; 50% of all employers in [jurisdiction] will voluntarily implement financial education that aligns with U.S. Treasury Department's Core Competencies; [Jurisdiction] will move 60% of all unbanked individuals into the financial mainstream with bank accounts and/or direct deposit within 5 years; [Jurisdiction] will reduce the foreclosure rate by 40% within the next 18 months.

7. Conduct and release an official research survey, study, or report on financial literacy and financial capability in your area

Leverage existing resources from states and other governments to determine which data is most critical in your jurisdiction. If resources are not available to conduct a unique study, leverage the state-by-state results from the FINRA Foundation's National Financial Capability Study. Usfinancial capability.org

8. Stay connected

Invite federal agencies, federal officials and statewide officials to partner with state, tribal or local campaigns. Establish relationships with consortiums such as Cities for Financial Empowerment, so that your Council can share and learn from others.

9. Be inclusive

Conduct "listening sessions" with local stakeholders such as youth, service providers, community organizations, employers, practitioners and others to better understand the issues and financial challenges faced by people in your community and to help drive and hone the Council's focus and energy.

The President's Advisory Council on Financial Capability would like to thank the following organizations for contributing their expertise, guidance and support in the creation of this document:

AARP Foundation
Accion Texas
Charles Schwab Foundation
Cities for Financial Empowerment Coalition
Corporation for Enterprise Development
Council for Economic Education
Defense Credit Union Council
Delaware's Office of Financial Empowerment
Economic Empowerment Initiative
Financial Education Network of San Francisco
FINRA Investor Education Foundation
Financial Literacy Center
Financial Literacy and Education Commission
Indianapolis Campaign for Financial Fitness
Jump$tart Coalition for Personal Finance
National Congress of American Indians
National Endowment for Financial Education
National League of Cities
Network for Teaching Entrepreneurship
New York Stock Exchange Foundation
Operation Hope
Society for Human Resources Management
United Way
U.S. Conference of Black Mayors
U.S. Department of Education
U.S. Department of the Treasury

Wisconsin's Office of Financial Literacy

The following cities and counties:
Chicago
County of Hawaii
Los Angeles
Miami
Newark
New York City
Providence
San Francisco
San Antonio
Savannah
Seattle

In: Federal Recommendations
Editor: Crystal M. Kirby
ISBN: 978-1-63117-038-6

Chapter 4

EVERY AMERICAN FINANCIALLY EMPOWERED: A GUIDE TO INCREASING FINANCIAL CAPABILITY AMONG STUDENTS, WORKERS AND RESIDENTS IN COMMUNITIES*

White House Staff

USING THIS RESOURCE GUIDE

The goal of this resource guide is to inspire leaders at all levels to leverage partnerships to create their own financial capability initiatives as a means toward building financial well-being for every American.

The **President's Advisory Council on Financial Capability** was created January 29, 2010, by Executive Order to advise the President and the Secretary of the Treasury on ways to empower Americans to better understand and address financial matters in order to improve their financial well-being.

Based on a review of the research on financial literacy, the Council decided to concentrate its final recommendations on three primary places financial education should be delivered in order to reach Americans throughout their lives: **school, workplace, and community.** This framework was used to organize this document.

---

* This white paper was released by the White House, May 2012.

"A Guide for City and Community Leaders to Create Financially Capable Communities" was written and released by the U.S. President's Advisory Council on Financial Capability in April 2012. This document supplements that work with resource guides for schools, institutions of higher education, and employers.

While research shows financial literacy is highly correlated with financial planning and that better planning leads to higher levels of wealth accumulation,[1] there are no universal standards to evaluate the quality and effectiveness of financial education programs and resources, particularly across diverse populations. As we initiate efforts to promote financial capability, **we urge every leader to help build the body of knowledge of what works** by testing and evaluating promising strategies.

This document is not intended to be exhaustive and does not create any requirements for schools, school districts, businesses, or communities, or other entities or individuals. While it provides many examples of financial capability initiatives around the country, this document is intended for reference only and is not intended to endorse or promote specific initiatives.

INTRODUCTION

Every American Financially Empowered

No issue is currently more important to this country than restoring economic security for all families in the wake of the greatest economic crisis since the Great Depression. From saving for retirement and higher education to better understanding credit card, student loan, and mortgage debt, personal financial decisions have important ramifications for families and children, as well as implications for our nation's economy. Financial capability means making informed and effective decisions about the use and management of money. This requires empowering every individual with the knowledge, skills, and access to tools to manage their finances effectively for long-term well-being.[2]

Low levels of financial capability are evident across the U.S. A 2009 Financial Industry Regulatory Authority (FINRA) survey of Americans revealed that about half report trouble keeping up with monthly expenses, have no money saved for emergencies and do not save for retirement.[3] Less than half, 41% of those surveyed, have no savings for their children's education.[4] Approximately 1 in 8 Americans are considered "unbanked" and do not access a bank or credit unit."[5] Research shows that low levels of financial literacy are associated with high levels of indebtedness, lower wealth accumulation, and less retirement savings. One example that signals a potential issue with indebtedness across the country is the ratio of debt to personal disposable income (household leverage), which increased from 55% in 1960 to 65% by the mid-1980s and escalated to 133% in 2007.[6]

Financial capability is especially low in certain populations. Young people, low-income households, Latinos and African-Americans show particular vulnerabilities in financial capability.[7] Approximately 1 in 3 Latinos and African-Americans are unbanked[8] and nearly a quarter approach retirement with less than $1,000 in total net worth, excluding pensions and Social Security.[9] Compared with U.S. national averages, young adults (ages 18-29) are more frequent users of non-bank borrowing (including payday loans and pawn shops), more likely to pay the minimum payment only on their credit cards, and more likely to be unbanked.[10]

Low financial literacy serves as a barrier to the middle-class. Research has shown a correlation between low financial literacy and financial choices that can block a low-income household's pathway to the middle class, including taking out high-cost mortgages, only paying the minimum credit card balance, and being delinquent on debt.[11] One study found that low-income households more frequently did not understand the terms of their mortgages, especially if the mortgages carried an adjustable rate.[12] Another study found that one-third of credit card charges and fees paid by consumers with low financial literacy were directly attributable to misunderstanding credit card contracts, with some costs totaling hundreds of dollars per year.[13] In addition, a lack of financial literacy also makes low-income households particularly vulnerable to predatory lending practices. For these households, the cost of low levels of financial literacy is high.

COMMUNITIES

A Guide for City and Community Leaders to Create Financially Capable Communities

Key Steps: Communities

Local leaders in states, tribes, local governments and communities play a critical role in helping people improve their financial capability. Because local leaders have a unique understanding of the economic, financial and educational obstacles that negatively impact the people in their communities, they are in a strong position to drive local strategies and initiatives that can make a real difference. Many states, tribes and local governments are already leading the charge to promote financial capability in their jurisdictions.

Successful states, tribes and localities leverage existing resources and infrastructure – and they utilize partnerships across the public, private and nonprofit sectors – to implement innovative programs that improve the financial well-being and outcomes of their citizens. They have clear objectives, well-defined program implementation and marketing strategies, and outcomes-driven metrics. Successful jurisdictions should also share their findings, best-practices, and challenges with other communities.

These steps were developed by the President's Advisory Council on Financial Capability (PACFC) and serve as a resource guide and a roadmap to help regional, state, tribal and local leaders get started with their own financial capability initiatives. The resources provided are intended to serve as examples, not exhaustive lists or endorsements, of those currently available.

Step 1: Assess the Local Landscape and Make a Case for Addressing Financial Capability

To build local support and develop working partnerships to advance financial capability in communities, stakeholders need to understand why financial capability is an important issue, what's currently being done in the community to address the issue, what's at stake in communities with poor financial health, and how strong financial behaviors and outcomes among community members can have a positive impact on a community's overall economic health.

❖ Begin by evaluating the current landscape.

Conduct an inventory of organizations and programs that are already involved with or are addressing financial empowerment initiatives, such as financial literacy and education, asset-building, financial coaching, tax-preparation assistance, and anything else related to financial capability. Keep in mind that many banks and foundations fund this type of work at the local level, so it may make sense to find out which initiatives have been successful, and include representatives from those initiatives in the discussion.

❖ Gather data to build the business case for a local financial capability initiative.

Key elements of a business case could include:

- Your state's performance on the FINRA Investor Education Foundation's National Financial Capability Study, where you'll find how your state compares to other states and the nation as a whole in five measures: spending vs. saving, emergency savings, non-bank borrowing, financial literacy, and comparison shopping.
- Your state's performance on the Corporation for Enterprise Development Assets & Opportunity Scorecard, a state-by-state performance and policy analysis in five areas: Financial Assets & Income, Businesses & Jobs, Housing & Homeownership, Health Care and Education.
- Local rates of "unbanked" / "underbanked" individuals, meaning the percent of individuals who do not have a bank or credit union account (unbanked), or may have an account with a mainstream financial institution, but turn to alternative financial service providers to fulfill their immediate financial needs (underbanked).
- Local foreclosure rates. Websites such as RealtyTrac can provide statistics.
- Local performance on financial capability among the general population and/or specific segments such as youth and workers. Local/state insights may be culled from national studies and resources, including:
- Employee Benefit Research Institute
- Gallup Hope Index
- Jump$tart Coalition for Personal Financial Literacy
- State-by-state results on the National Financial Capability Challenge
- Information and testimonials about how other communities have embraced financial capability and improved the financial well-being of their citizens. Some examples include Delaware, Wisconsin, New York City, San Francisco, Indianapolis, San Antonio, Seattle-King County, Savannah, Providence, American Indian and Alaska Native Tribes, and many others. (See Appendix: Communities beginning on page 14.)

Step 2: Create a Local Council

A local financial literacy / financial capability council is a formalized group of influential individuals representing governments, education leaders, nonprofit organizations, academia, private foundations, and private industry who agree to serve voluntarily with the collective goal of enhancing financial literacy and capability among the state, tribe or local community.

Potential benefits of creating a local council:

- **Builds efficiency** by sharing information and resources across multiple organizations with similar goals.
- **Encourages innovation** by bringing unique points of view and areas of expertise to the table.
- **Helps communities set strategic priorities** through collaboration and cross-institutional partnership.
- **Maximizes resources by pooling human and financial capital** to jointly solve problems and minimize duplicative programs in local areas.
- **Creates greater visibility and cross-community support** by helping to ensure that resources are focused where the impact can be greatest.

❖ **Determine who should be a part of the Council.**

Councils can take many shapes and sizes. In fact, it's critical that they be customized to the unique needs and circumstances of the local community. Members of the President's Advisory Council on Financial Capability held meetings and learning sessions with state and city councils and leaders to identify common practices that lead to successful local efforts. Through those discussions, several common themes and recommendations emerged.

By and large, experts agree that councils can be most effective when they include influential leaders and decision-makers.

Cities for Financial Empowerment

Cities for Financial Empowerment (CFE) brings together pioneering municipal governments from across the country that have begun to use their power and positions to advance innovative financial empowerment initiatives.

Members have made tangible and measurable commitments to supporting financial empowerment programming in their cities, and are now joining together to both teach and learn from one another. By working with key partners in the public, private, and nonprofit sectors, CFE also leverages its members' collective power to advance the financial empowerment agenda on a state and national level. Most recently, Bloomberg Philanthropies and Living Cities announced a $16.3 million investment to replicate the evidence-based financial empowerment model to cities across America.

Consider the following:

- Government leaders, both elected and high-level career staff, who can prioritize public resources and leverage a "bully pulpit" to improve visibility and awareness of the issues and solutions.
- Education leaders, including school superintendents and school board members, who can effect change within the existing education infrastructure and among local youth.
- Financial education experts, including nonprofit and community-based organizations, professional associations, Cooperative Extension services and others with expertise in delivering financial education and capability content. Examples include the Financial Planning Association (FPA), the National Association of Personal Financial Advisors (NAPFA) and the Association for Financial Counseling, Planning and Education (AFCPE).
- Nonprofit organizations, libraries, and other community service providers with expertise serving specific populations such as youth, underserved individuals and low- to moderate-income families.
- Academics and researchers, who bring extensive knowledge, data, and objective analysis of what works and what does not work in promoting financial capability.
- Local business leaders, particularly those from financial institutions such as banks and credit unions, who bring business and financial acumen, product-development expertise, and financial and professional (pro bono) resources.
- Local community members who may be struggling with financial instability themselves, or who may offer practical insights on the issues and concerns of community members.

- Other stakeholders who can share unique perspectives, such as youth leaders, retirees, and other engaged residents.

❖ Identify a leader for the Council.

Identify a leader or official within the jurisdiction who has the mandate, influence, and stature in the government and community to lead the Council effort. (For example, in San Francisco the effort is led by the City Treasurer; in New York City, the effort is led by the Commissioner of the Department of Consumer Affairs.)

❖ Recruit Council members.

Identify influential government officials and/or elected officials, representatives of businesses (both financial and non-financial), non-profit organizations, academic institutions, private foundations and other individuals who are willing and eager to engage on the topic of financial literacy, capability, and empowerment.

❖ Take official steps to create the Council.

This could mean encouraging legislation to create the Council or encouraging state, county or city executive branch leaders to create it by executive order. See Appendix: Communities beginning on page 14 for examples of executive orders.

❖ Formally kick off the Council.

Host a preliminary hearing and/or meeting in your area around the "State of Financial Literacy and Financial Capability." Announce the establishment of the Council and its charter.

STEP 3: Focus the Work and Establish Goals

❖ **Determine key areas of focus for the jurisdiction's financial capability work and then establish committees or working teams to be responsible for each area of focus.**

Each jurisdiction will have unique priorities. However, the President's Advisory Council on Financial Capability recommends three broad areas that will be relevant to any community:

1) Youth financial education and capability,
2) Financial access for the underserved, and
3) Financial capability through the workplace.

❖ Articulate clear goals and metrics.

Create a core list of financial literacy and financial capability goals and objectives that will enhance the lives of community members.

The following is a sample, non-comprehensive list of example goals and metrics:

- Every public school student in [jurisdiction] will have the opportunity to complete financial capability education;
- 50% of all employers in [jurisdiction] will voluntarily implement financial education that aligns with U.S. Financial Literacy Education Commission Core Competencies;
- [Jurisdiction] will move 60% of all unbanked individuals into the financial mainstream with bank accounts and direct deposit within 5 years; and
- [Jurisdiction] will reduce the foreclosure rate by 40% within the next 18 months.

Step 4: Build Momentum

❖ **Conduct and release an official research survey, study, or report on financial literacy and financial capability in your area.**

Leverage existing resources from states and other governments to determine which data is most critical in your jurisdiction. If resources are not available to conduct a unique study, leverage the state-by-state results from the FINRA Foundation's National Financial Capability Study.

❖ **Stay connected.**

Invite federal agencies, federal officials and statewide officials to partner with state, tribal or local campaigns. Establish relationships with consortiums such as Cities for Financial Empowerment, so that your Council can share and learn from others.

❖ **Be inclusive.**

Conduct "listening sessions" with local stakeholders such as youth, service providers, educators, community organizations, employers, practitioners and others to better understand the issues and financial challenges faced by people in your community and to help drive and hone the Council's focus and energy.

Step 5: Develop and Launch Programs that Address the Stated Goals

Consider adopting some of the following programs and initiatives, many of which have been successfully implemented in other jurisdictions. The initiatives are organized under the PACFC's three core areas of focus: financial education for youth, financial capability in the workplace, and financial capability and access for the underserved.

Increasing Access to Financial Aid

With dedicated "post-secondary coaches" at John Hancock High School in Chicago, students were helped to access about $3.5 million in scholarship grants and financial aid in 2010, up from $5,000 just a few years earlier. The school's college enrollment rate has also increased from 49 percent in 2008 to more than 80 percent in 2010.

❖ **Consider financial education for youth and students.**

- Encourage and/or incentivize your school district to develop a K-12 plan providing options for schools to integrate curriculum that is aligned with what young people need to know, at what ages, in order to become financially capable.

- Resources to support these plans, as well as information concerning state mandates and local resources, can be found at Jump$tart Coalition and the Council for Economic Education websites. "Money as You Grow'" is another useful resource that provides 20 financial lessons and associated activities for children ages 3 to 18+.
- Encourage public schools to establish programs to ensure all students have the knowledge necessary to undertake financial planning for college and career goals, and specifically for college-bound students to ensure that they understand the FAFSA form, reduce their exposure to higher-interest private loans, and maximize their capture of federal loans. The U.S. Department of Education FAFSA website provides resources.
- Encourage and/or incentivize local high schools to participate in the National Financial Capability Challenge, which raises awareness about the need for financial capability efforts and is sponsored by the U.S. Department of Treasury. Participating students and schools are eligible for scholarships and grants.
- Ensure that youth summer jobs provided by the state, tribe or local government incorporate direct deposit, savings accounts, and financial capability and financial literacy training. The Economics Awareness Council in Chicago implemented such an initiative. Resources to help local governments integrate financial literacy into summer jobs programs are available from the United States Conference of Mayors DollarWI$E Campaign.
- Encourage local youth-services organizations to adopt programs that deliver financial education. Examples include:
  - Boys & Girls Clubs of America's Money Matters: Make It Count
  - Junior Achievement
  - Boys Scouts and Girls Scouts personal finance badges

See the Guide for K-12 (page 17) and Higher Education (page 28) for additional resources and considerations.

❖ Consider financial capability and access for the underserved.

Reduce the number of unbanked individuals in your community.

BankOn programs are partnerships typically between banks/credit unions, community partners and government entities to provide access to low-cost, safe accounts and financial education for unbanked and usually low-income individuals. The BankOn website provides state, tribal and local data on the un- and under-banked and many resources on starting a Bank On initiative, as well as the ability to participate in discussions with other Bank On leaders.

- Conduct an assessment of your community's needs and identify local barriers to financial stability for residents. Consider evaluating the number of unbanked individuals, as well as whether and why individuals are using "alternative" banking services such as pay-day lenders and check-cashing services. This information will help inform the types of programs, products and services that may be needed in your community.
- Set targets for improving financial capability in your community – and focus on addressing the needs and/or problems you identified in your assessment / evaluation.
- Establish an awareness campaign and/or website to keep the local conversation growing and to provide tools to parents and families. For examples, see Delaware's $tand by Me and Indianapolis's Indy Campaign for Financial Fitness.
- Support an area-wide (state, tribe, city) Earned Income Tax Credit (EITC) campaign to help low-income workers learn how to access their benefits.
    - Corporate Voices for Working Families offers free employer guides and EITC educational and marketing toolkits. Some examples from cities that have implemented EITC programs are Los Angeles and Washington, D.C.
- Support initiatives to provide financial education at teachable moments. For example, some cities are incorporating FAFSA help with tax assistance provided at IRS offices for national VITA (Voluntary Income Tax Assistance) coalitions.
    - Ladder Up is an organization that demonstrates how this can work in practice.

❖ **Consider financial capability in the workplace.**

- Draft formal recommendations that your state, tribal or local government adopt employee benefits / workplace financial capability programs for its own employees.
- Host meetings and/or summits with state, tribal and local employers and encourage the adoption of employee benefits.
- Encourage local employers to compete in the Workplace Leaders in Financial Education Awards, sponsored by the American Institute of Certified Public Accountants (AICPA) and the Society for Human Resources Management (SHRM).
- Schedule a workshop on retirement plan options with the U.S. Department of Labor's Employee Benefits Security Administration and the AICPA to learn about the available options and how to start a plan.
- Encourage attendance at educational events sponsored by the U.S. Department of Labor and Internal Revenue Service's (IRS) Employee Plans Division to help small and mid-size businesses understand their responsibilities in operating a retirement and/or health benefits plan.

PACFC Recommendations for the Federal Workplace

- Identify a set of standards and metrics for measuring success.
- Create a centralized location for financial capability resources.
- Create a consistent ongoing awareness campaign.
- Create an expert "speakers bureau."
- Utilize data from existing surveys to target efforts and measure impact.
- Read more.

❖ **Consider other initiatives.**

The following ideas and initiatives may support more than one of the core areas of focus listed above (youth, access for the underserved, and workplace):

- Create Financial Education Networks, whereby local nonprofits, educators, practitioners, librarians, government leaders and others are able to become familiar with areas of expertise and programming, and find opportunities to share best practices and maximize local

resources. San Francisco and New York City provide Financial Education Network information and resources:
  - San Francisco
  - New York City
- Be inclusive and further encourage partnerships by hosting financial literacy town hall meetings, roundtables, conferences, and listening sessions to share ideas, collaborate, and explore new ways to enhance local financial capability. See an example of a press release announcing a listening session in Indianapolis.
- Create a local "financial literacy corps" that provides a centralized local resource for information on financial literacy volunteer opportunities across the state/tribe/city.
- Build interest in your work by leveraging existing public awareness campaigns, such as:
  - National Financial Capability Month
  - Money Smart Week
  - America Saves Week

Step 6: Measure Your Impact and Adjust Accordingly

As with any successful initiative, it's critical to establish at the outset clear objectives, as well as clear milestones, benchmarks and metrics for measuring success (See Step 3). Consider whether the chosen goals are implementable and achievable, given economic realities and conflicting pressures for time and money.

If initiatives fall short of achieving the established goals, carefully evaluate which factors or elements of the program to adjust. Reconsider whether the goals themselves are realistic for your community. And regardless of whether you're meeting all your goals, be sure to share your findings and results with other jurisdictions so they can learn from your experience.

National Endowment for Financial Education's research-based customizable Evaluation Toolkit offers methods to measure program impact.

Appendix: Communities

- **Choosing a Retirement Solution for Your Small Business:** Choosingaretirementsolution.org A jointly sponsored interactive website from the U.S. Department of Labor and the AICPA to help small businesses find retirement plan options appropriate for their business and access to more in-depth information on what is involved in establishing and operating each of the options.

- **Cities for Financial Empowerment Coalition**: cfecoalition.org
  The Cities for Financial Empowerment brings together pioneering municipal governments that use their power and positions to advance innovative financial empowerment initiatives.
- **Corporation for Enterprise Development:** cfed.org
  CFED programs test and refine promising ideas to find out what works. Programs include matching funds, IDAs, asset-building for children, and self-employment tax initiative. In addition, the CFED Scorecard reviews state-by-state performance and policy measures across five areas: Financial Assets & Income; Business & Jobs; Housing & Homeownership; Healthcare and Education. Scorecard: cfed.org/scorecard/
- **Council for Economic Education:** councilforeconed.org/
  CEE offers comprehensive K-12 economic and personal finance education programs, including the basics of entrepreneurship, consisting of teaching resources across the curriculum, professional development for teachers, and nationally-normed assessment instruments.
- **Delaware's $tand by Me program:** standbymede.org
  The Delaware Financial Empowerment Partnership (DFEP) is a joint venture of the State of Delaware and the United Way of Delaware, providing a package of financial empowerment services called $tand By Me.
- **Financial Education Network of San Francisco:** frbsf.org/community/issues/fensf.html The Financial Education Network-San Francisco (FEN-SF) is a collaborative group of San Francisco's nonprofit service providers, philanthropic funders, and local public sector representatives dedicated to improving financial education services in the City.
- **Financial Literacy Center/New York Stock Exchange Foundation:** nyse.nyx.com/financial-fitness-kit
  NYSE Foundation and the Financial Literacy Center provide free resources for employers and employees.

- **U.S. Financial Literacy and Education Commission:** mymoney.gov Free, unbiased resources from more than 20 federal agencies on array of financial topics.
- **FINRA National Financial Capability Study**: http://www.finrafoundation.org/web/groups/foundation/@foundation/documents/foundati on/p120535.pdf
  The FINRA Investor Education Foundation commissioned this national study of the financial capability of American adults. The overarching research objectives were to benchmark key indicators of financial capability and evaluate how these indicators vary with underlying demographic, behavioral, attitudinal and financial literacy characteristics.
- **First Nations Development Institute:** www.firstnations.org
  Provides financial education training to Native communities and tribal governments.
- **Gallup Hope Index:** www.operationhope.org/page/pgid/39
  Measures financial literacy in relationship to hope, wellbeing, and engagement among U.S. students in grades 5 through 12.
- **Indianapolis Campaign for Financial Fitness:** indyscampaign.org
  ICFF is a coalition of public and private organizations that helps Indianapolis residents and their families manage their finances. The goal is to achieve the improved quality of life that accompanies financial stability at any income level.
- **Join Bank On**: JoinBankOn.org
  Research your community's under- and un-banked stats, and learn how to start a Bank On program in your area.
- **Banking On Opportunity: A Scan of the Evolving Field of Bank On Initiatives:**
  This document provides an overview of the Bank On concept, defined as an initiative in which low-cost transaction and savings accounts are made available to unbanked individuals by federally insured banks and credit unions. http://www.treasury.gov/resource-center/financial-education/Documents/Banking%20On%20Opportunity%20Nov%2011.pdf
- **Jump$tart Coalition for Personal Finance:** jumpstart.org
  Jump$tart is a national coalition of organizations dedicated to improving the financial literacy of pre-kindergarten through college-age youth by providing advocacy, research, standards and educational resources.

- **Money As You Grow:** moneyasyougrow.org/
  Money As You Grow is a new, online tool that provides 20 essential financial lessons that kids need to know as they grow. They're written in easy-to-understand language, aimed at parents and children, and organized into 4 key concepts per age group.
- **National Congress of American Indians**: ncai.org
  Works with tribal leaders on training and technical assistance on significant issue areas including financial education. Also conducts a Tribal Exchange on the Stock Market.
  Native Initiatives Community Development Financial Institutions (CDFI): http://www.cdfifund.gov/whatwedo/programsid.asp? Prog ramid=3 Coalition of more than 69 members to help strengthen the Native Community Development Financial Institution industry through which a significant amount of financial education for Native communities takes place
- **National Endowment for Financial Education – Consumer and Educator Resources:** NEFE offers consumer resources, an interactive video sharing site, a high-school financial planning program, and site dedicated to community financial education instructors.
  - Smart About Money, a site that provides practical articles, worksheets, tips and valuable resources to help users understand and manage money: http://www.smartaboutmoney.org/
  - High School Financial Planning website: http://hsfpp.nefe.org
  - Spendster, an online site that allows the public to share their purchasing experiences and learn from one another: http://spendster.org/
  - Financial Workshops: http://www.financialworkshopkits.org/
- **National Endowment for Financial Education – Resources for Employers:** retirementtlc.org
  NEFE provides employers with a research-based step-by-step process to increase retirement savings plan participation, particularly among low-income and female employees.
- **National Financial Capability Challenge:** challenge.treas.gov
  Information about the National Financial Capability Challenge, a financial capability test for high-school students sponsored by the U.S. Department of Treasury and U.S. Department of Education.
- **National League of Cities**
  Bank On Toolkit for Municipalities: Nlc.org/

- **SHRM and AICPA's Workplace Leaders in Financial Education Awards:** Wlife.org
  Awards program that recognizes organizations with exemplary workplace financial literacy efforts to enhance employee financial well-being and encourages employers to implement and further develop financial literacy programs.
- **United Way:** unitedway.org/our-work/income/
  In 2008, United Way initiated an ambitious 10-year plan to cut in half the number of lower-income families who are financially unstable. This site provides information about how local United Way organizations are helping drive financial stability in their communities.
- **United States Conference of Mayors DollarWI$E Campaign**: http://usmayors.org/index.php/dollarwise/summer-youth-campaign/
  Provides resources for local governments to include financial literacy in summer youth jobs programs.
- **Wisconsin Governor's Council on Financial Literacy:** wdfi.org/ymm/govcouncilfinlit Link to the Executive Order establishing the Council: wdfi.org/resources/indexed/site/ymm/govcouncilfinlit/ExecOrder24.pdf

Additional resources are available in K-12, Higher Education, and Workplace Sections of this document.

K-12 Schools

A Guide to Increasing Financial Capability among Students in K-12 Schools

Key Steps: K-12 Schools

The vast majority of Americans (82%) believe personal finance should be taught to all students at least as early as high school.[14] However, only 13 states have some type of personal finance course requirement for graduation and just 9 states have formal requirements to assess students' financial literacy.[15] While the curriculum varies by state, financial education typically covers basic household decision-making concepts such as budgeting, credit, compound interest, and investment options. Some states require students to receive instruction in an independent class, while others allow required instruction to be incorporated into existing classes, offer instruction as an elective, or provide a curriculum to districts that they could choose to implement. Recognizing that not all families are able to provide the adequate financial guidance to their children, school, college and community efforts can level the playing field for all future consumers and entrepreneurs.

Providing financial education may change students' financial behavior over time. The Jump$tart Coalition for Personal Financial Literacy conducted biennial tests of the financial literacy of high school seniors from 1997 to 2008. One study shows that while a high school course on money management or personal finance did not increase college students' scores on the Jump$tart test, the course did improve certain financial behaviors such as credit card repayment and checking account balancing.[16] The results of this research suggest that financial education is best viewed as a long-run investment requiring sustained effort, rather than a short-term fix. In addition, financial education curricula that incorporate real-world experience in budgeting, credit management, and financial products appear more promising than those that do not.

Throughout this chapter we provide resources for financial education in K-12 schools. These resources are intended to serve as examples, not exhaustive lists or endorsements, of those currently available. Whether financial education already is taught in your classrooms or you are just getting started, this resource guide will help you begin to evaluate your current state, implement programs, and measure results.

Step 1: Assess the Local Educational Environment

❖ **What is the current state of personal finance instruction in your school or school district?**

Key questions to answer during this process are:

- What is being taught and when?
- In what subject area(s), specific class(es), and grade(s) is it being taught?
- Who is teaching personal finance concepts and what are their qualifications in this content area?
- What training and support is offered for teachers?
- What resources/curricula are they using?

- How is instruction delivered (e.g. lecture, classroom activity, workshop, guest presenter, tour, simulation, etc.)?
- Where do the learning experiences occur (e.g. classroom, club activity, workshop, online, simulation, event, etc.)?
- What is the length of instruction (e.g. one-time event over two days, semester course, one class period per week throughout the semester, etc.)?
- Are learning experiences coordinated across subjects, departments or grades?
- How is learning assessed?
- Does current data that provides a snapshot of the financial capability of past or current students?
- Is the financial education experience required or an elective?

❖ **What, if any, non-school extra-curricular activities address financial education for youth in your community?**

All education groups in a community should work collaboratively to plan consistent and sequential delivery of content. Programs focused on youth should be encouraged to coordinate efforts to prevent redundancy and to avoid gaps. For example, a student could learn about budgeting from multiple teachers and youth mentors but potentially never learn about the value of risk management and insurance if efforts are not coordinated.

Examples of national nonprofit organizations with financial education activities include Girl Scouts and Boy Scouts, Boys and Girls Clubs, 4-H, and Junior Achievement.

Where to look for non-school personal finance activities might include:

- School-sponsored after-school programs
- State agencies, commissions, or other entities focused explicitly on financial capability
- Community or faith-based youth groups and programs
- Parent organizations
- Financial institutions
- Other local/state government or community initiatives

❖ **What personal finance standards, personal finance requirements, and testing requirements already exist in your state? How do they relate to other education standards in your state?**

Key questions to answer during this process are:

- How does your district currently address local and state personal finance state-specific personal finance requirements?
- Are there existing local grade-level or graduation expectations in personal finance?
- What, if any, state and local credentialing/licensing are required to teach personal finance? What criteria are used to determine who teaches personal finance in your district?
- What resources are available for instruction related to standards and requirements?

An example resource to help answer this question includes the Survey of the States by the Council for Economic Education.

❖ Is financial education being delivered in local and state colleges and universities, including 2-year colleges?

Key questions to answer during this process are:

- In what form(s) do local post-secondary institutions offer financial education?
    - Courses (required/elective)
    - Degree programs
    - Exposure through Financial Aid office
    - Freshman or new student orientation
    - Student centers with resources, peer-to-peer, etc.
- Are there opportunities for your pre-K-12 school/school district to:
    - Coordinate your financial education offerings for a meaningful sequence of learning throughout a student's education?
    - Prepare your students for a smooth transition to topics covered in post-secondary school?
    - Encourage meaningful repetition of concepts and avoid needless repetition?
- Do your local colleges and universities accept high school personal finance or similar courses to satisfy admission requirements, and/or offer dual enrollment course credit?

Step 2: Build a Team

❖ Create a voluntary, temporary or permanent task force or advisory council with members who share the collective goal of promoting financial education in your school or district.

Key questions to answer during this process are:

- Using the information gathered in Step 1, what will be the purpose and goal(s) of the team? Will it focus on strategic planning, fundraising, program implementation, support for teachers, measurement, advocacy, etc.?
- How will you design the team composition to meet stated goals?
- How will the team be held accountable for success?

❖ **Include representation from within and outside the school/district, ensuring top-level support.**

Consider including:

- Teachers and department chairs who will carry out the program;
- Education leaders who can effect change within the existing education infrastructure;
- Non-school youth program personnel, if your program will occur outside of the school or complement school activities;
- Members from existing school-private/non-profit partnerships;
- State, city, local stakeholders who promote financial capability (e.g. Local Financial Capability/Literacy Councils);
- Representatives from local higher education institutions;
- Representatives from local financial institutions such as credit unions, banks, insurance organizations, etc.;
- Representatives from other local small businesses;
- Financial services professionals;
- Parents, parent organizations, and other community stakeholders; and
- Students.

❖ **Recognize the potential benefits of creating a collaborative team and consider ways to foster a collaborative culture.**

Key considerations are:

- Choose a proven, strong leader who can help create buy-in, visibility, and advocacy.
- Create clear processes to coordinate efforts inside and outside schools.
- Select team members with broad expertise.
- Provide other resources as needed, e.g., a venue for an after-school program.

Step 3: Define the Problem and Set Program Goals, Objectives, and Metrics

❖ **Gather data that describes the problem and helps focus efforts.**
  - Identify the need for increased financial capability.
  - Share the data describing the problem, as appropriate, and communicate the objectives to the school/district community to establish shared responsibility.

Examples of resources to help answer this question include:

- State-by-state results on the National Financial Capability Challenge
- Jump$tart Coalition for Personal Financial Literacy
- See additional resources for community data on page 7.

❖ **Review any existing state and district standards and evaluate standards developed by relevant organizations as a guide for establishing district priorities for financial capability.**

Please note: There are no *national* education standards or curricula mandated by the U.S. Government. The following examples have been developed by non-federal entities.

Examples of resources:

- Voluntary National K-12 Content Standards in Economics by Council for Economic Education
- National Curriculum Standards for Social Studies – Economics by National Council for the Social Studies

- National Standards for Business Education – Personal Finance by National Business Education Association
- National Standards for Family and Consumer Sciences Education by Consumer and Family Resource
- Standards for Entrepreneurship Education by Consortium for Entrepreneurship Education
- National Standards in K-12 Personal Finance Education by Jump$tart Coalition for Personal Financial Literacy

❖ Articulate clear overarching goals and metrics for assessment.

- Create a core set of financial literacy and financial capability goals that provide clear benefits if met.
- Consider using SMART (Specific, Measurable, Attainable, Relevant, Time-bound)[17] goals or some other strategic framework to set clear, actionable targets.

The following is a sample, non-comprehensive list of example goals and metrics:

- By 20XX, 100% of our students will complete the FAFSA, complete at least three college applications, and comparison shop for colleges based on awarded grants and scholarships to find the best value.
- Every student in our district will have a savings account by Grade X, with a minimum of X saved for college.
- Our school, or every public school in our district, will have financial capability education in place by 20XX.
- Every public school student in [jurisdiction] will complete financial capability education upon graduation, beginning with the class of 20XX.

Step 4: Design the Strategy and Define the Curriculum/Program

❖ **Determine how personal finance will be integrated into learning opportunities.**

Key questions to answer during this process are:

- What are the best models and programs for teaching and learning financial capability, and could they be adapted for our students?
- Will programs be offered as new stand-alone classes or integrated into other course offerings(s)?
- Will programs be offered during the regular school day, or as an opportunity out of school?

❖ **Identify specific learning outcomes and benchmarks to drive decisions for the school or district about personal finance education. Consider how these outcomes will be integrated into a school or district's success outcomes.**

Examples include:

- A fourth grade student can explain the difference between buying with cash and buying with credit cards.
- An eighth grade student can list actions to take to protect one's personal identity information.
- A twelfth grade student can explain how interest, fees, and grace periods affect credit card costs.
- The President's Advisory Council on Financial Capability's "Money as You Grow" tool identifies 20 key lessons for youth and parents as children develop.
- Examples of proposed standards in Step 3 have additional benchmarks for consideration.

❖ **Select or develop curriculum that aligns with learning outcomes and school or district expectations.**

Examples of resources provided by the non-profit and government sectors include:

- One example of a statewide financial education implementation can be found in the Smart Tennessee financial literacy program, which featured public-private partnership and positive assessments. It provides school districts with one framework for personal finance content and training.

- Lessons related to spending, saving, borrowing, and protecting against risk can be found at National Financial Capability Challenge Educator Toolkit.
- The Federal Deposit Insurance Corporation (FDIC) has designed "Money Smart for Young Adults," an eight-module financial education program for youth aged 12 to 20.
- The Network for Teaching Entrepreneurship (NFTE) offers curriculum, "Entrepreneurship: Owning Your Future," and many other resources.
- Jump$tart's Clearinghouse, an inclusive online library of financial education resources, and Jump$tart's Best Practices, a resource for use when developing and or selecting personal finance education materials.

Key questions to answer during this process are:

- Are resources readily available to teachers and learners?
- Do the resources and curriculum align with the designated local learning outcomes and established state and national frameworks?
- Are resources provided by credible resources in a noncommercial manner?
- Are resources accurate and up-to-date?
- Are web-based resources accessible using the technology and software available in the local schools and libraries?
- What is the cost of materials (initial cost, sustainable cost, additional costs to implement)?
- Are there any restrictions on use of open-source resources or no-cost materials?
- Are materials age-appropriate?
  - Does the curriculum allow for customization to the target group and personalization for each student (i.e. English Language Learners (ELLs), students in Individualized Education Programs (IEPs), or of different cultural backgrounds)?
- Are materials available in other languages, audio, large print, or Braille?
- Is the curriculum interactive and experiential, using real-life practice and implementation to encourage active learning?
- Do the materials include assessment tools to help instructors measure student progress?

❖ **Determine whether or not the coursework will be recognized by a post-secondary school for admissions/credit.**

When higher education institutions recognize personal finance courses for admissions/credit, it broadens the opportunity for high schools to promote the advantages of financial education across the entire student body. Students are more likely to take a course that satisfies some type of college requirement.

Step 5: Focus on Instruction and Instructors

Teachers from diverse backgrounds are being tapped to teach financial education topics that they may know very little about. A two-year national study conducted by the University of Wisconsin-Madison[18] found that teachers need and would welcome more formal education on financial literacy.

The study found that formal education is a predictor of teachers' own perceived competence to teach specific topics. Although 89 percent of K-12 teachers agree that students should either take a financial education course or pass a competency test for high school graduation, less than 20 percent feel competent to teach financial education topics, and 63.8 percent feel unqualified to use state financial literacy standards. Positively, more than 70 percent say they are willing to get formal financial education training.[19]

These steps outline how to ensure instruction is delivered by qualified and credible teachers who are well-prepared and confident to teach personal finance.

❖ Establish guidelines and/or requirements for instructors.

Key questions to answer during this process are:

- What credentials, qualifications and/or experience must your teachers have to teach personal finance for their grade level and teaching assignment?
- Do you have tiers for personal finance instructor qualifications, i.e., are the requirements appropriate for the grade/level being taught?
    - Can educators be classified into tiers of expertise or credentials (e.g., minimum requirement, ideal)?

- Have you established guidelines or protocols for non-school-system staff (co-teachers, guest speakers, support instructors, volunteers, etc.) who deliver personal finance programs to youth, such as:
  - Keeping their presentation noncommercial (i.e., they do not sell products or services to the students);
  - Adhering to school regulations for proper conduct (e.g., keeping student information confidential); and
  - Ensuring they are qualified and credible in the context of delivering financial education.

❖ Establish a system for providing training so instructors are prepared to teach personal finance with an appropriate level of mastery of the topics, instruction methods, and with confidence.

Key questions to answer during this process are:

- How are instructors assigned to teach personal finance?
  - What are their qualifications to teach personal finance?
  - Are there gaps in their knowledge that need to be filled? Do they need new or refresher training?
- What training will be provided/offered to personal finance teachers?

Ideally that training should:

- Be sufficient in quality, intensity, and duration to lead to improvements in instructional practice;
- Be developed to include content as well as instruction methods and practices to meet stated instructional goals;
- Provide opportunities for collaboration among teachers;
- Be adaptable to be delivered in multiple venues: in person, online, distance learning, etc.; and
- Be eligible for Continuing Education Units (CEUs)

Some examples of training programs can be found here:

- Family Economics and Financial Education Training, University of Arizona
- National Institute of Financial and Economic Literacy, State of Wisconsin

Step 6: Implement

Put your plan into place. Whether you roll out all at once or one program at a time, develop a work plan and include processes/mechanisms to monitor the program(s) progress. Assign members of your team the responsibility for oversight of the implementation and monitoring.

Step 7: Evaluate Results and Adjust Accordingly

As with any successful initiative, it is critical to establish at the outset clear objectives, as well as clear milestones, benchmarks and metrics for measuring success (see Step 3). Consider whether the chosen goals are implementable and achievable, given economic realities and conflicting pressures for time and money.

If initiatives fall short of achieving the established goals, carefully evaluate which factors or elements of the program to adjust. Reconsider whether the goals themselves are realistic for your school or school district. And regardless of whether you're meeting all your goals, be sure to share your findings and results with other jurisdictions so they can learn from your experience.

The National Endowment for Financial Education's research-based customizable Evaluation Toolkit offers methods to measure program impact.

Where feasible, help grow the body of knowledge of what efforts are effective in promoting financial capability by conducting a rigorous evaluation of interventions. This should include a treatment group and a control/comparison group and involve a research/evaluation office or partner to ensure validity of the research design.

Appendix of Resources: K-12 Education

State-by-State Status of Personal Finance and Related Education

- Council for Economic Education 2011 Survey of the States: http://www.councilforeconed.org/news-information/survey-of-the-states/

- Jump$tart's State Financial Education Requirements Map: https://www.jumpstart.org/state-financial-education-requirements.html

Research

- Financial Industry Regulation Authority (FINRA) Financial Capability Study: http://www.usfinancialcapability.org/

Sample Standards

- Financial Education: https://www.jumpstart.org/national-standards.html
- Social Studies: http://www.socialstudies.org/standards
- Economics: http://www.councilforeconed.org/wp/wp-content/uploads/2012/03/voluntarynational-content-standards-2010.pdf
- Business: http://www.nbea.org/newsite/curriculum/standards/index.html
- Consumer Science: http://www.pafcs.org/fcs-standards
- Entrepreneurship: http://www.entre-ed.org/Standards Toolkit/

Core Competencies

- U.S. Financial Literacy Education Commission Financial Education Core Competencies: http://www.challenge.treas.gov/educatortoolkit/documents/Core Competencies.pdf

Sample Teaching and Learning Resources

- American Federation of School Administrators (AFSA) Money Skill (free): http://www.moneyskill.org/
- Council for Economic Education (CEE) Financial Fitness for Life (varies, free-cost): http://www.councilforeconed.org/resources/type/classroom-resources/
- Everfi's Financial Literacy Platform for High Schools (free to public high schools): http://www.everfi.com/for schools.php
- FDIC Money Smart for Young Adults: http://www fdic.gov/consumers/consumer/moneysmart/young.html

- National Endowment for Financial Education (NEFE) High School Financial Planning Program: http://www.hsfpp.org/
- Take Charge America Institute (TCAI) Family Economics and Financial Education (FEFE): http://fefe.arizona.edu/about-fefe
- Visa's Practical Money Skills for Life: http://www.practicalmoneyskills.com/foreducators/
- Wells Fargo's Hands on Banking: http://www.handsonbanking.org/en/educators.html

Support Resources and Programs

- U.S. Financial Literacy and Education Commission's MyMoney.gov Website: http://www.mymoney.gov/index.html
- "Money As You Grow": money milestones and activities geared for youth ages 3 to 18+: www.moneyasyougrow.org

Examples of Topic-Specific Resources

- Econedlink: http://www.econedlink.org
- Network for Teaching Entrepreneurship's "Entrepreneurship: Owning Your Future: http://www.nfte.com/resources/buy-resources
- The Stock Market GameTM:http://www.smgww.org

Case Studies

- Smart Tennessee Financial Literacy Program: http://www.smarttn.org

Program Evaluation Resources

- National Endowment for Financial Education Evaluation Toolkit: http://toolkit.nefe.org

Preparation for Higher Education (See Guide and Appendix for Higher Education)

- College Navigator, U.S. Department of Education, online search tool to help prospective students select where to apply: http://nces.ed.gov/collegenavigator/

- College Scorecard, White House and U.S. Department of Education, Online snapshot of key value metrics to help prospective students select where to apply: http://www.whitehouse.gov/issues/education/scorecard

HIGHER EDUCATION

A Guide to Increasing Financial Capability among Students in Higher Education

Key Steps: Institutions of Higher Education

Compared with U.S. national averages, young adults (ages 18-29) are more frequent users of non-bank borrowing (including payday loans and pawn shops), more likely to pay the minimum payment only on their credit cards, and more likely to be unbanked.[20] Every year, nearly 2 million low- and moderate-income undergraduates do not submit a Free Application for Federal Student Aid (FAFSA) to apply for federal financial aid, even though many of them are eligible for Pell Grants, which they would not have to repay.[21] Seventy-five percent of students who apply for federal aid are unable to comparison shop for colleges based on actual financial aid award offers because they only list a single school on the FAFSA.

While college has never been more important, it has also never been more expensive. For the first time, Americans owe more debt on their student loans than they do on their credit cards. Students who damage their credit scores by defaulting on their student loans are less likely to secure employment because of credit checks as criteria for employment and they may face challenges in investing in a home or starting a business.

This brief guide is meant to be a resource for campus leaders as they begin to develop plans for improving students' financial capability. While this section focuses primarily on students, postsecondary institutions may also want to address the financial capability needs of faculty and staff (See "A Guide to Increasing Financial Capability among Employees in the Workplace") and consider ways to contribute to increasing the financial capability of the broader community beyond the gates of the institution through research, teaching, and service.

Step 1: Assess Existing Efforts to Improve Financial Capability

❖ What is the current state of efforts to improve financial capability on your campus?

Key questions to answer during this process are:

- What is happening, who is involved, and what is known about results of financial capability efforts?
- What is required for students and what is optional?
- What are the qualifications of individuals leading these efforts and what is known about their effectiveness?
- What training and support is offered for instructors and program leaders?
- To what extent are financial capability efforts happening and coordinated across different departments and offices?
- How does your institution collaborate with K-12 education and other partners in this area?
- How do we facilitate education and counseling efforts, as well as other strategies such as disbursing financial aid in ways to minimize fees students pay and hosting Volunteer Income Tax Assistance sites to increase FAFSA completion and education tax credit uptake been considered?

Step 2: Build a Team

❖ **Create a campus-wide voluntary, temporary or permanent task force or advisory council with members who share the collective goal of increasing financial capability and well-being.**

Key questions to answer during this process are:

- Using the information gathered in Step 1, what will be the purpose and goal(s) of the team? Will it focus on strategic planning, program design and implementation, support for instructors and staff, measurement of results, etc.?
- How will you design the team composition to meet stated goals?
- How will the team be held accountable for success?

❖ Include representation from across the institution, ensuring top-level support.

Consider including:

- Trustees
- President and Provost
- Offices of admissions and financial aid
- Bursar
- Academic deans and departments
- Professors
- Offices of student life and residence life
- Health center
- Greek life and athletics
- Student government and student organizations
- Offices of alumni relations and career services
- Institutional research office
- Parents

❖ Identify potential external partners.

The right partners will support efforts to increase college students' financial capability.

Other partnerships, such as K-12 schools, family support organizations, and research centers, may provide opportunities for the institution to conduct research or ways to coordinate community education on financial matters.

Consider engaging:

- K-12 schools
- Curriculum providers
- Financial institutions
- Non-profit, community, and/or faith-based organizations
- Local/state government

Step 3: Define the Problem and Set Program Goals, Objectives, and Metrics

❖ Identify the specific financial decisions faced by current, former, and prospective students, as well as others beyond campus.

A list of examples of specific financial decisions faced by current, former, and prospective students can be found on page 34.

❖ Gather baseline data that describes the problem and informs objectives.

- Identify national, state, district, or school indicators of the need for increased financial capability.
- Consider gathering student-specific data, for example from a financial health assessment upon enrollment, student focus groups, course grades and follow-up surveys from a personal finance course, or student aid records, to allow for personalized efforts and provide a baseline for tracking results. Any method must comply with privacy laws.
- Share the data describing the problem, as appropriate, with the school/district community to establish shared responsibility.

❖ Articulate clear goals and identify metrics for assessment.

- Create a core list of financial capability goals that if attained will mean improved financial decision-making and financial well-being for students and others
- Consider using SMART (Specific, Measurable, Attainable, Relevant, Time-bound)[22] goals or some other strategic framework to set clear, actionable targets.
- Consider taking a "student success" approach and working with students themselves to identify what they need to be financially successful.
- Share the goals with the college community to establish shared responsibility.

The following is a sample, non-comprehensive list of example goals and metrics:

- By 20XX, 100% of our students complete the FAFSA each year and exhausts Federal aid before taking private loans.
- Every student uses direct deposit for work-study jobs and student loan credit balances by 20XX.
- Every student receives education tax credits for which they are eligible by 20XX.
- By 20XX, every student selects optimal loan repayment plan, repays loans, and avoids default.

Step 4: Design the Strategy and Determine the Initiative's Components

❖ Identify a range of possible components of the strategy and determine which are most likely to be effective.

A list of example activities, tools, and efforts to promote financial capability among current, former, and prospective students follows this section can be found on page 35.

Key questions to answer in this process are:

- What are we already doing that demonstrates results and should continue?
- What are we doing that does not demonstrate results and should end or be changed?
- Which efforts are most likely to align financial capability objectives with overall educational objectives such as retention, completion, and job placement?
- What do sub-groups of students, such as veterans, students with disabilities, low-income students, or first-generation college students, need to be financially successful?
- How do socio-cultural, emotional, and psychological factors affect financial decisions and how can you design efforts with behavioral economics in mind?
- How will you design structural elements of the strategy – such as providing aid award letters in machine-readable format or opening

federally-insured deposit accounts for students – in addition to counseling and education efforts?

- How will the strategy focus both on avoiding financial trouble and building wealth?
- How will you make learning activities experiential and appropriately sequential?
- How and at what time do you provide one-on-one counseling and coaching in addition to any other efforts?
- What efforts will focus on engaging students through peer-to-peer counseling, work-study opportunities, or service-learning projects connected to academic courses?
- What efforts are specifically designed to ensure professional instructors are appropriately trained and/or credentialed and receive regular feedback to improve their effectiveness?
- How will we build capacity of professionals by training appropriate faculty and staff?
- What is our commitment to contribute to the evidence base for improving financial capability by evaluating campus, community and K-12 programs using an experimental or quasi-experimental approach, and by conducting other research?

See examples of Institutions of Higher Education promoting financial capability on page 37.

Step 5: Implement

Put your plan into place. Whether you roll out all at once or one program at a time, develop a work plan and include processes/mechanisms to monitor progress. Assign members of your team the responsibility for oversight of the implementation.

Step 6: Evaluate Results and Adjust Accordingly

As with any successful initiative, it is critical to establish at the outset clear objectives, as well as clear milestones, benchmarks and metrics for measuring success (see Step 3). Consider whether the chosen goals are implementable and achievable, given economic realities and conflicting pressures for time and money.

If initiatives fall short of achieving the established goals, carefully evaluate which factors or elements of the program to adjust. Reconsider whether the goals themselves are realistic for your institution. And regardless of whether you're meeting all your goals, be sure to share your findings and results with others so they can learn from your experience.

Where feasible, help grow the body of knowledge of what efforts are effective in promoting financial capability by conducting a rigorous evaluation of interventions. This should include a treatment group and a control/comparison group and involve the institutional research office or appropriate faculty and graduate students. Institutions without a research mission could partner with some other research institution.

What Financial Decisions Do Students Face?

This list provides examples of specific financial decisions faced by current, former, and prospective students.

Prospective Students

- Saving for college
- Comparing colleges before applying using College Navigator, College Scorecard, net price calculators, and other tools
- Applying to multiple colleges to permit comparison shopping
- Applying for scholarships that do not need to be repaid
- Submitting a completed FAFSA to be eligible for federal student aid
- Comparing financial aid packages to select the best value program

Current Students

- Whether to borrow and how much to borrow over entire academic program, not just one year at a time
- How many credits to take and how long to take to complete the program

- Planning career paths and estimating likely earnings after completion
- Submitting a completed FAFSA to be eligible for federal student aid
- Exhausting federal aid before taking private loans
- Whether and how much to work (Federal Work-Study or some other job)
- Opening safe, affordable, federally-insured deposit accounts and avoiding fees
- Making an academic plan and a spending plan and sticking to them (understanding relationships between the pace of academic progress and financial aid eligibility, the total cost of a certificate or degree, and earnings tradeoffs)
- Comparison shopping for course materials
- Managing loan refunds (i.e. credit balances) responsibly
- Paying student loan interest while in school so it doesn't capitalize
- Paying bills on time and using credit cards responsibly
- Filing tax returns without fees and receiving eligible tax credits, such as the American Opportunity Tax Credit (AOTC)
- Building a strong credit score and avoiding adverse action on credit reports
- Preparing to make decisions about student loan repayment
- Preparing for career-related decisions such as seeking employment, negotiating salary and benefits, choosing a health insurance plan, saving and investing for retirement, making charitable contributions, weighing transportation and housing costs, interpreting pay statements and understanding taxes, etc.

Former Students

- Making career-related decisions such as those listed above
- Choosing optimal student loan repayment options, repaying loans, and avoiding student loan defaults
- Making donations to support their alma mater
- Using credit responsibly, building a strong credit score to earn favorable borrowing rates
- Saving and investing to build wealth while reducing risk through diversification
- Purchasing adequate insurance

Activities to Promote Financial Capability among Students

This list provides examples of activities to consider when creating a strategy to promote financial capability among current, former, and prospective students.

Help prospective college students make sound decisions about postsecondary education.

- Make net price calculators easy to find
- Provide aid award offers consistent with forthcoming model aid award format from U.S. Department of Education and allow students to download their award letters in machine readable format
- Provide tools for students to understand likely full cost to degree and total expected debt and monthly loan payments for different amounts of time to degree
- Partner with middle and high schools to support and evaluate instructional methods, train teachers and guidance counselors, and place work-study students as financial counselors and college advisers to help with FAFSA completion, scholarship searches, and financial planning.

Help current students identify and meet their academic and financial goals.

- Help students make and stick to a well-defined 2-year or 4-year academic and financial plan
- Use indicators of academic or financial challenges – attendance, grades, dropped classes, no books, late payments, etc. – to target interventions
- Help students plan career paths using actual and projected wage data

Consider curricular and co-curricular opportunities for financial education and counseling.

- Provide enhanced, personalized loan counseling for all student loan borrowers

- Integrate financial topics into developmental Math and English and first-year success courses and assess students' financial readiness
- Offer required or optional credit-bearing courses and certificates
- Infuse financial topics across the curriculum, not only in personal finance courses
- Show films about finances as part of a series of campus events and workshops
- Provide opportunities for students to learn about money on their own by linking to unbiased financial management games, tools, and information sites
- Use text messages and social media to send timely, actionable messages
- Require students who manage budgets (e.g. student government, student organizations) to demonstrate financial competencies

Consider policies/programs beyond financial education that improve financial capability.

- Open safe, affordable federally-insured deposit accounts for students unless they opt out of receiving one; use for student aid balances and work-study payments
- Make sure accounts or federally-insured pre-paid cards have best possible terms for students – lowest fees, strong consumer protections
- Host a student-run Volunteer Income Tax Assistance site for students, staff, and community members to get free help with preparing tax returns and completing the FAFSA
- Ensure students regularly update their contact information with loan servicers to reduce the likelihood they default on loans because they cannot be contacted

Engage students in experiential activities

- Provide financial counseling internship, work-study, and service-learning opportunities for students in academic programs related to financial empowerment and entrepreneurship, such as education, social work, and business

- Train students to act as financial counselors to peers, K-12 students, and community members
- Involve students as research assistants on financial capability research and evaluation projects

Conduct research and evaluation to build the evidence base

- Partner with K-12 schools and community organizations to help them understand the effectiveness of their financial capability efforts
- Evaluate campus programs and share results with other colleges

Appendix of Resources: Higher Education

- **U.S. Department of Education College Navigator**: http://nces.ed.gov/collegenavigator/
- **White House and U.S. Department of Education College Scorecard**: http://www.whitehouse.gov/issues/education/scorecard
- **Federal Student Aid, U.S. Department of Education Default Prevention Resource Information**: http://ifap.ed.gov/Default PreventionResourceInfo/
- **Federal Deposit Insurance Corporation (FDIC) "Money Smart and Money Smart for Young Adults"**: http://www.fdic.gov /consumers/consumer/moneysmart/index.html
- **Federal Student Aid, U.S. Department of Education Student Aid on the Web "College Prep Checklist"**: http://studentaid.ed.gov
- **Consumer Financial Protection Bureau Student Debt Repayment Assistant**: http://www.consumerfinance.gov/students/
- **U.S. Department of Labor, Employee Benefits Security Administration**: www.dol.gov/ebsa. Several resources for college seniors including Time Is On Your Side and Savings Fitness – A Guide to Your Money and Your Financial Future, videos as well as webcasts on key financial steps.
- **U.S. Department of Labor, Women's Bureau Wi$e Up: Financial Planning for Generation X & Y Women**: http://wiseupwomen. tamu.edu/index.php
- **American Institute of Certified Public Accountants 360 Degrees of Financial Literacy**: http://www.360financialliteracy.org/

- **Operation HOPE Banking On Our Future, College Edition**: http://www.operationhope.org/banking-on-our-future-college
- **The University of Arizona Family Economics and Financial Education**: http://fefe.arizona.edu/
- **National Endowment for Financial Education Cash Course**: http://www.cashcourse.org/
- **FINRA Investor Education Foundation MoneyTopia** (for military families): http://www.saveandinvest.org/MilitaryCenter/P124790
- **LoveYourMoney,** University of Tennessee Extension – Department of Family and Consumer Sciences. Free, online financial education resource for students: http://loveyourmoney.org/

Examples of College Efforts to Improve Financial Capability

Center for Financial Literacy

Champlain College, VT

The Center is a partnership between several Vermont financial institutions and Champlain College. It aims to increase financial literacy in classrooms across Vermont, ensure college students graduate with the skills to make sound decisions about spending, credit and investments, and help adults navigate difficult financial situations such as buying a home and saving for retirement. The Center has hosted K-12 teacher training workshops for Vermont teachers and partnered with a local bank to help college students access and understand their credit scores.

Center for Financial Security

University of Wisconsin, WI

Founded by the School of Human Ecology, the Center focuses on applied research that promotes individual and family financial security and aims to inform public policy about financial issues on a local, state, and national level. Researchers and graduate students investigate how to measure financial security and literacy, determine target audiences for interventions to improve financial security and literacy, and which interventions work. The Center's interactive "Financial Security Index" tool presents users with a short questionnaire that concludes with a snapshot of performance on financial knowledge, attitude, and behavior measures.

Credit-Wise Cats

Arizona State University, AZ

Trained students serve as personal finance ambassadors to local schools and the community in the Tucson area. Each year the Credit-Wise Cats host the Arizona Financial Face-Off for teams of high school students who have participated in personal finance workshops to compete for cash prizes based on their financial knowledge.

Dollars and Sense

James Madison University, VA

"Decision-making in a Modern Society," is a 3-credit course that reaches 1,500 first-year students each year. It uses real-life scenarios to give students practice making financial decisions through simulations. "Dollars and Sense" is a practical course that reviews the effect of personal philosophy on money, influences of societal expectations, and management of personal finances, and is open to parents, high school counselors, and others through the outreach and engagement office. Each semester, in "Getting Your Financial Ducks in a Row," faculty and staff across the university receive training to develop their own financial skills that they are expected to pass along these lessons to students they come in contact with. JMU also offers a 7-week non-credit course in partnership with the VA Society of CPAs and has recently formed a Personal Financial Education Committee composed of students, staff, and faculty to develop a comprehensive plan for helping students improve their financial health.

Financial Aid U

Essex County College, NJ

In partnership with the Newark Now Financial Empowerment Center, the National Community Tax Coalition Financial Aid U initiative, and the IRS Volunteer Income Tax Assistance program, Essex Community College provides free tax preparation and FAFSA completion services to reduce the number of students who pay fees for these services and to increase the number of students who receive all tax credits – including education tax credits – and student aid for which they are eligible.

Financial Life at OSU

The Ohio State University, OH

OSU views financial well-being as part of overall student wellness. In addition to providing students with links to tools like a credit card payoff and cost of living calculators, the university offers financial education and counseling services through Scarlet and Gray Financial, which is housed at the Student Wellness Center in the Office of Student Life. Peer educators use Twitter and Facebook to send students financial tips, provide downloadable information sheets for residence halls, and offer personal advising on a variety of financial topics.

Financial Literacy Research Center

Dartmouth College, NH, and University of Pennsylvania, PA

A partnership among RAND, Dartmouth, and the Wharton business school at the University of Pennsylvania (Penn), the Center develops and tests innovative programs to improve financial literacy and improve financial decision-making. Projects include financial planning videos for young adults and instructional materials on financial matters embedded in quantitative literacy courses for pre-service K-8 teachers.

Financial Literacy Seminar Series

George Washington University, DC

The Financial Literacy Seminar Series, a joint initiative between the Board of Governors of the Federal Reserve System and the George Washington University School of Business, brings together academics, practitioners, policy makers, and other experts to present and discuss research on financial literacy.

Personal Financial Planning Program

Texas Tech University, TX

The Personal Financial Planning program, part of the College of Human Sciences, offers undergraduate and graduate certificates and degrees in personal financial planning. In addition, all students have an opportunity to develop healthy financial behaviors through the Red to Black outreach program that aims to empower students through financial counseling, coaching, and training. The Center for Financial Responsibility conducts research on topics such as cultural and gender issues in personal finance and individual investor behavior.

Powercat Financial Counseling

Kansas State University, KS

Students studying to become financial professionals are paid to provide free, one-on-one financial counseling to their peers, both in person and via

Skype. Students also deliver presentations on financial topics to the campus community. A student advisory board shapes the goals of the center, and social media are used to connect students to the center.

WORKPLACE

A Guide to Increasing Financial Capability among Employees in the Workplace

Key Steps: Employers

American employers are a trusted source of financial education for their employees. Providing financial education opportunities at the workplace, where there is a direct connection with earnings and benefits, can be a powerful way to inform financial decision-making. While the research on the methods to promote financial capability is evolving, more than a decade of research suggests that financial education efforts in the workplace are important to reducing financial stress, increasing workplace productivity, and promoting long-term financial well-being.

Effective financial education programs can improve employee finances. One study of a workplace education initiative in Omaha and Kansas City found that this program increased the use of budgets, reduced late payment of bills and reported delinquency, lowered credit card balances and increased the frequency of carrying no credit card balance at the end of the payment cycle. Additionally, this program significantly reduced the number of loans from 401(k) programs, produced a marked increase in retirement saving accounts and401(k) take-up.[23] The participating companies in the initiative were diverse, including a large financial company, a health care establishment, a restaurant, and a retail enterprise.

Improved employee finances can improve employers' bottom line. Researchers have demonstrated a link between financial stress and days of work missed; in addition, financially stressed workers tend to spend more time at work handling personal finances.[24] One study found that 15 percent of American workers experience financial stress to such a degree that it impacts their productivity.[25] Another study found that financial stress is significantly linked to personal and work satisfaction.[26] Workers with low levels of financial stress tend to miss work less and are more productive while at work.

Offer a retirement plan to improve employee financial security. Offering a retirement plan can be one of the most challenging, yet rewarding, decisions an employer can make. The employees participating in the plan, their beneficiaries, and the employer benefit when a retirement plan is in place. Administering a plan and managing its assets, however, require certain actions and involve specific responsibilities. To meet their responsibilities as plan sponsors, employers need to understand some basic rules, specifically the Employee Retirement Income Security Act (ERISA). ERISA sets standards of conduct for those who manage an employee benefit plan and its assets (called fiduciaries). For more information, see the U.S. Department of Labor's publication entitled Meeting Your Fiduciary Responsibilities.

As employers play a critical role in helping people improve their financial capability, the goal of this guide is to inspire businesses and corporations to serve as a trusted delivery point for financial education and related benefits. The resources provided are intended to serve as examples, not exhaustive lists or endorsements, of those currently available.

While we do not have all the answers, significant research has illuminated effective strategies and mechanisms to improve employee financial decision-making. We therefore offer a roadmap to help employers create financial capability initiatives with specific guidance in four key areas:

- Payroll & Benefits
- Education &Training
- Marketing & Communication
- Measuring Impact & Reporting Results

Step 1: Assess Your Company's Efforts to Promote Financial Capability

Use the Employer Checklist (page 47) to begin assessing company efforts to empower employees to make positive financial decisions.

Step 2: Articulate Specific Measureable Goals and Identify Related Metrics

- What are your goals related to a 401(k) or equivalent plan (e.g., to increase participation, raise contributions rates, support sound investing and achievement of retirement income security)?

- What are your most important goals related to the overall financial well-being of employees (e.g. credit card debt, investments, financial stress level, etc.)?
- As an employer, how do chosen financial wellness goals relate to an overall strategy for worker productivity, attracting and retaining talent?
- What specific metrics relate to your overarching financial capability goals?

The following is a sample, non-comprehensive list of example goals and metrics:

- Every employee will participate in our retirement savings plan, contributing a minimum of 3% of pay by 20XX.
- By 20XX, employees that retire from our company will feel and be more financially secure.
- By 20XX, every parenting employee will have dedicated savings accounts for college for his or her children.
- Every employee who faces major life events, such as buying a home or expecting a child, will receive unbiased, affordable personalized one-on-one financial counseling or other effective financial planning support by 20XX.

Step 3: Introduce Effective Mechanisms Related to Payroll & Benefits

Proven mechanisms can help drive behavioral change. Studies have documented that it is human nature to be overwhelmed by complex decision-making and put off long-term benefits for short-term gain.[27] Financial decisions about retirement saving, investments, and insurance are no different. However, several strategies are proven to help drive behavior change.

❖ Learn from examples of exemplar employee benefit programs.

Resources to support these types of efforts can be found at:

- Employee Benefit Research Institute provides information about employee benefits programs and public policy.

- Learn about your options for providing a retirement savings plan at choosingaretirementsolution.org or retirementmadesimpler.org

❖ Introduce effective mechanisms to promote participation in retirement savings.[28]

- **Defined Benefit Pension Plans:** These plans automatically cover all eligible employees, and, by relying on professionally pooled investment management and by pooling longevity risk, efficiently and effectively deliver retirement security. Backed by government guarantees, the plans can provide secure retirement income for life.
- **Defined Contribution Savings Plans:** These plans can also deliver retirement security, especially if designed to promote participation, adequate contributions, sound investing, and efficient translation of savings into retirement income.
- **Auto-Enrollment and Company Matching:** Too many employees fail to participate or save enough in available 401(k) plans. Employers can help bring workers into the retirement saving universe by assisting employees to overcome administrative barriers to saving. Automatic enrollment in retirement savings accounts has a material impact on the participation rate on new hires, with one prominent study estimating that automatic enrollment increases new hire participation in 401(k) plans by 38.5 percentage points.[29]

Key questions to answer during this process are:

  - Will you offer automatic enrollment to all employees or just new hires? What about part-time workers?
  - Will you offer a company match? If so, at what rate?
  - When will you allow employees to change their participation?
  - How will you ensure transparency in the process?
- **Default Contribution Rate:** Employees who are automatically enrolled in a workplace retirement savings plan typically maintain the default contribution rate, making the employer's decision about the default contribution rate all the more important. Studies have shown that the primary effect of selecting a higher default contribution rate is to increase contributions and that a high default contribution rate has little impact on participation.[30]

Key questions to answer during this process are:

- Understanding that the research suggests that a high default contribution rate has little impact on participation,[31] what rate will the company set as the default during auto-enrollment?
- At what times will you allow employees to change the rate at which they contribute?
- Will you vary the default based on employee factors such as years to retirement?
- How will you ensure transparency in the process?

❖ **Introduce effective mechanisms to grow retirement savings appropriately.**[32]

- **Automatic Escalation:** Automatic escalation of a retirement plan is beneficial because it increases employee contribution to the retirement plan by automatically increasing the proportion saved over time or from annual salary increases and/or promotions. Auto-escalation of savings can be expected to increase employee retirement saving contributions, especially for low-income workers. One study estimates that the automatic escalation feature may increase overall 401(k) accumulations by 11-28% in the lowest income quartile and 5- 12% for those in the highest income quartile.[33] This approach helps overcome the downsides related to the initial lower contribution rate.
- **Default Investment Fund:** Just as employees typically maintain the default contribution rate, employees often keep their contributions invested in the default portfolio investment fund. Employers can help workers grow their retirement contributions over time by selecting a default investment fund with appropriate risk for each employee.
- **Consider instituting low-cost target date funds (TDFs), which account for varying levels of employee risk.**[34]
  A TDF is an investment fund that automatically resets the asset mix (stocks, bonds, and cash equivalents) in its portfolio according to a predetermined path over a selected time frame. Participants may hold on to the investment as part of their retirement savings portfolio after they retire, but the investment's name typically includes a year at or near when people investing are expecting to retire. A TDF for an older worker about to retire (such as a "2015 Fund") would typically have a lower percentage of equities in its asset mix and more bonds or cash

equivalents (considered a less risky portfolio), while a TDF for a younger worker (such as a "2060 Fund") will have a higher percentage of equities and less bonds or cash equivalents (considered a higher risk portfolio).

The Pension Protection Act of 2006 instituted safeguards for employers who select TDFs as default investments for employees. A growing number of recently hired participants in 401(k) retirement plans—particularly those in their 20's— are investing in target-date funds (TDFs), according to an analysis by the Employee Benefit Research Institute (EBRI). In 2006, 28.3% of recently hired (those with two or fewer years of tenure) 401(k) participants held TDFs, and as of 2010 it has risen to 47.6% according to EBRI.

The Employee Benefit Security Administration of the U.S. Department of Labor has guidance on default investments, target date funds, and related disclosures for workers in 401(k) plans.

- **Consider offering annuities or other mechanisms that help workers translate savings balances into secure retirement income streams.** As life expectancies and retirement periods lengthen, Americans are increasingly confronting the risk of outliving their assets in retirement. Managing this risk is a challenge. While we know average life expectancies, it is impossible for individuals to know how long they will live. As a result, many retirees risk outliving their savings or unnecessarily limiting their spending in retirement because of the fear of outliving their savings. Women are especially exposed to this risk. Traditionally, a guaranteed and predictable stream of lifetime income, such as a defined benefit pension, has helped to attenuate this risk, for both men and women. Lifetime income could also be provided by an annuity purchased through a 401(k) or IRA.

❖ Introduce effective mechanisms to link employees to federally-insured financial institutions.

- Paper Free Checking with Direct Deposit: Employers that offer direct deposit with federally-insured financial institutions can help their employees build a relationship with a financial institution that is advantageous in regards to borrowing and decreasing the pressure or need to borrow against the company pensions. Being a customer of a federally insured financial institution makes it possible to utilize their financial services, such as IRA or other saving instruments that can further help employees save for retirement. Direct deposit also often provides employees with benefits such as free checking accounts and lower minimum balances. It is also safer because it removes the risk of the check getting lost in the mail, while simultaneously reducing an employer's administrative costs.

Step 3: Initiate Financial Education & Training Efforts

Many individual financial decisions—for example, choice of health care benefits and retirement planning—are made with employer assistance. Accordingly, employers are in a unique position to understand how and why employees make financial decisions and to provide guidance.

❖ Develop a financial health assessment that will enable employers and employees to design a customized benefit plan.

Employees will be able to utilize an assessment to make them better prepared to deal with their personal finances going forward, which can help make them reduce financial stress in the long run.

❖ Identify and engage strong external partners that share your stated goals of promoting financial capability.

Consider:

- Non-profit and community organizations;
- Faith-based organizations;
- Local/state/federal government;
- Financial institutions; and
- Educational institutions that can support research and evaluation efforts.

$tand By Me

An example of how business, government and nonprofits can work together, $tand By Me is a partnership between the State of Delaware, United Way, and local employers to provide one-on-one financial coaching in participating Delaware workplaces.

$tand By Me financial empowerment centers are co-located within public agencies, non-profit organizations, and businesses who embrace shared goals of reaching and serving Delawareans who want to take charge of their financial future.

❖ **Provide financial information and training about the company's benefits and financial education topics like budgeting, saving, borrowing, and protecting one's identity and investments.**

Resources to support these types of efforts can be found at:

- Society for Human Resources Management / American Institute of Certified Public Accountants – Workplace Leaders in Financial Education Award
- NYSE / Financial Literacy Center Workplace Financial Fitness Kit
- National Endowment for Financial Education Financial Workshops
- Savings Fitness: A Guide to Your Money and Financial Future and Taking the Mystery Out of Retirement Planning from the U.S. Department of Labor

Examples of financial education topics include:

- Your Financial Fingerprint: Understanding Personal Financial Data
- Managing Cash Flow
- Planning for Taxes
- Making Retirement a Reality
- Maximizing Company Benefits
- Understanding Inflation
- Buying a Home
- Supporting Elderly Parents
- Making Major Purchases
- Choosing Investments Wisely[35]

❖ **Get creative.**

While effectively delivered seminars and workshops can significantly improve financial decisionmaking,[36] research also indicates individuals respond to new, innovative strategies to deliver key financial lessons.

Staples

Staples has partnered with Doorways to Dreams Fund (D2D) to create—“Staples” Bite Club-- a financial education game that encourages employees to improve their retirement savings. Staples chose to use D2D’s *Bite Club*, a vampire game, in order to appeal to hourly retail employees as well as employees newly eligible for the 401(k) plan. This innovative approach engages employees using the cutting-edge game frame to improve personal financial capability, self-confidence and knowledge. In 2012, Staples won an Eddy Award from *Pensions and Investments* for its use of video games to make retirement saving, budgeting and planning fun.

❖ **Customize your approach to meet the needs of your employees.**

- **Customize benefits:** An increasing number of potential employees are giving significant weight to the employee benefits offered by an employer. Customized employee benefits can attract and retain talent. Employee retention is positively influenced by customized benefits packages, as employees will not want to lose their customized benefits. Customization also increases employee appreciation of company benefits.
- **Develop high quality and low cost benefit plans**: Use new service provider fee transparency requirements issued by the U.S. Department of Labor on pension plan service provider fees and investment expenses to help develop high quality and low cost pension and 401(k) plans for employees.
- **Tailor communication:** Evidence indicates that employee subgroups, such as the young, women, and near-retirement employees, benefit from communication or programs that are specifically designed for them.
- **Factor in major life events:** Evidence shows that as employees undergo major life transitions, such as the birth of a child, the death of family member, or higher education investment employees can show less productivity due to stress and adjustment. Specific information and counseling around life events can foster smoother transitions during an employee’s career.
- **Involve employees:** Employers and educators should formally and informally ask employees about the financial tools and benefits that

interest them, and then design tailor-made programs for their employees.

Step 4: Create a Robust Marketing & Communication Strategy

- ❖ Craft specific and targeted messaging that is relevant to employees and integrates financial wellness into an overall employee wellness strategy.

Research shows that the employers that have been most successful at increasing their firm's employee participation rate did so by crafting specific and targeted messaging that would be relevant to the audience and integrated financial wellness into an overall employee wellness strategy that may include physical and mental health. The financial needs of employees vary greatly depending on their life stage. As a result, it is imperative to use marketing strategies that will resonate with the target audience, increasing the probability of participation in a program.

- ❖ **Encourage executives and managers to communicate a coordinated message about financial well-being.**

It is imperative to get buy-in from senior leadership to establish a financial education program. Irma Marias, an FDIC Community Affairs Specialist, says, "A workshop can help draw attention to the availability of financial education workshops and show their importance."[37]

Step 5: Measure Impact and Report Results

- ❖ Identify financial impact data to collect.[38]

Utilizing your measurable goals (established in Step 2) to determine what data is relevant to the employer's key stakeholders.

Examples are:

- Federal Insurance Contribution Act (FICA) expenses
- Flexible spending account (FSA) participation
- Worker productivity

- Financial security of retirement-eligible employees
- Survey data regarding credit card debt and monthly payment behaviors

❖ **Gather the financial impact data and conduct an impact analysis.**

Most data can be obtained from the compensation and benefits department. When data is difficult to collect, make reasonable estimates and be prepared to explain your reasoning and assumptions.

Employer Checklist

Payroll & Benefits

- **Offer improved retirement saving incentives,** such as a company match on 401(k) contributions.
- **Lower barriers to retirement saving** by adopting auto-enrollment, with pro-saving features such as auto-escalation of contributions, and auto-investment in default target-date funds.
- **Help employees access financial services** by referring them to appropriately vetted institutions.
- **Offer workers a direct deposit feature** to help qualify employees for other benefits such as a free checking account or a lower minimum balance.
- **Negotiate preferred pricing** for third party goods and services, such as phone services, hotels, and rental cars.

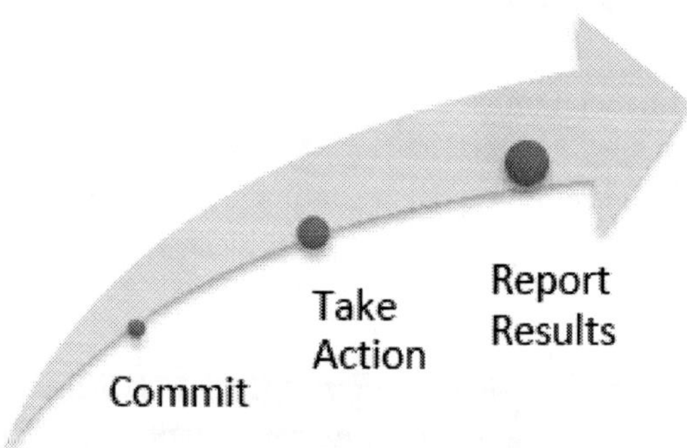

Education & Training

- **Design and offer a financial health assessment** that allows employees to assess their financial condition.
- **Offer courses and seminars in the basics of financial management**, focused on such topics as budgeting, saving, debt management, insurance, investing, and retirement planning.
- **Develop customized financial tools and investment education** for employees to individualize their retirement plans.
- **Inform and educate employees about potential tax-related benefits,** such as the Child and Dependent Care tax credit.

Marketing & Communications

- **Create an internal communication strategy** that actively encourages employees to take advantage of company-sponsored financial capability tools.
- **Engage employees' families** to ensure lasting change in financial habits.
- **Facilitate peer-to-peer sharing** of financial management tips.
- **Deliver targeted financial information on employee milestones**, such as birthdays, employment anniversaries, or changes in family status.
- **Encourage executives and managers to communicate with employees** about the value of financial capability tools.

Report Results

- Set specific, measurable goals for employee financial capability and frequently track employees' progress, providing assessments at least annually.
- Dedicate staff and budget resources to tracking results.

Appendix of Resources: Employers

- **Employee Benefit Research Institute,** Resources to support the development of sound employee benefits programs and public policy: www.ebri.org
- **Internal Revenue Service Retirement:** IRS.gov/retirement Online resources on choosing and maintaining retirement plans, including pension, profit-sharing, and 401(k) plans, 403(b) annuities, and IRAs, for plan sponsors, practitioners, and individuals.
- **National Endowment for Financial Education,** Resources on how to plan and deliver financial workshops financialworkshopkits.org
- **National Endowment for Financial Education,** Beginner's guide to financial readiness: smartaboutmoney.org
- **NYSE / Financial Literacy Center Workplace Financial Fitness Kit,** Online resources for employers and employees: nyse.nyx.com/financial-fitness-kit
- **Retirement resources** for employees: myretirementpaycheck.org
- **Society for Human Resources Management /American Institute of Certified Public Accountants Workplace Leaders in Financial Education Award**, recognizing companies and institutions for exemplary financial literacy efforts: http://www.wlife.org
- **$tand by Me – Delaware**, A partnership between the State of Delaware, United Way, and local employers providing 1:1 financial coaching in participating Delaware workplaces: standbymede.org
- **U.S. Department of Labor "Savings Matters,"** Online resources to help employees, regardless of age or career, understand retirement savings options and to help employers, whether a large company or small business, with questions about options as well as employer responsibilities: http://www.savingmatters.dol.gov/
- **U.S. Department of Labor and SEC Guidance on Target Date Funds**: http://www.dol.gov/ebsa/pdf/TDFinvestorbulletin.pdf.

End Notes

[1] Lusardi, Annamaria, 2003. "Planning and Saving for Retirement." Dartmouth College Working Paper. Lusardi, Annamaria and Jason Beeler, 2006. "Savings Between Cohorts: The Role of Planning." Michigan Retirement Research Center Working Paper.

[2] Executive Order 13530 - President's Advisory Council on Financial Capability (January 29, 2010). http://www.whitehouse.gov/the-press-office/executive-order-presidents-advisory-council-financialcapability

[3] FINRA Investor Education Foundation, National Survey of the Financial Capability Study, 2009. (http://www.finrafoundation/capability)

[4] *Ibid.*

[5] *Ibid.*

[6] Federal Reserve Bank of San Francisco, 2009. "U.S. Household Deleveraging and Future Consumption Growth." Online: http://www.frbsf.org/publications/economics/letter /2009/el2009-16.html

[7] Lusardi A. and Mitchell O., 2008. "How much do people known about economics and finance?" University of Michigan Retirement Research Center. http://www.ftc.gov/be /workshops/mortgage/articles/lusardimitchellum2008.pdf

[8] *Ibid,* FINRA National Survey on Financial Capability

[9] Lusardi, 2005. "Financial Education and the Saving Behavior of African-American and Hispanic Households." Dartmouth College. http://www.dartmouth.edu/~alusardi/Papers /EducationAfrican%26Hispanic.pdf

[10] *Ibid,* FINRA National Survey on Financial Capability.

[11] Gerardi, Kristopher, Lorenz Goette, and Stephan Meier. 2010. "Financial Literacy and Subprime Mortgage Delinquency: Evidence from a Survey Matched to Administrative Data." Working Paper No. 2010-10. Atlanta, GA: Federal Reserve Bank of Atlanta; Stango, Victor, and Jonathan Zinman. 2008. *Debit vs. Credit: How People Chose to Pay.* Madison, WI: Filene Research Institute; Lusardi, Annamaria, and Peter Tufano. 2008. "Debt Literacy, Financial Experience, and Overindebtedness." Dartmouth College Working Paper. Hanover, New Hampshire: Dartmouth College.

[12] Bucks, Brian, and Karen Pence. 2006. "Do Homeowners Know Their House Values and Mortgage Terms?" Washington, DC: Federal Reserve Board of Governors.

[13] Lusardi, Annamaria, and Peter Tufano. 2008. "Debt Literacy, Financial Experience, and Overindebtedness." Dartmouth College Working Paper. Hanover, New Hampshire: Dartmouth College.

[14] Practical Money Skills for Life, 2011. "Personal Finance Course Should be a High School Graduation Requirement." "http://www.practicalmoneyskills.com/resources/pdfs/Financial EducationSurvey0411.pdf

[15] Council for Economic Education, 2011. "A Survey of the States: Economic, Personal Finance & Entrepreneurship Education in Our Nation's Schools in 2011." http://www.councilforeconed.org/news-information/survey-of-the-states/

[16] Mandell, Lewis, 2009. "The Impact of Financial Education in High School and College On Financial Literacy and Subsequent Financial Decision Making." Presented at the American Economic Association Meetings in San Francisco, Calif., January 4, 2009.

[17] Dora, G. T.,1981. "There's a S.M.A.R.T. way to write management's goals and objectives." Management Review, Volume 70, Issue 11(AMA FORUM), pp. 35-36.

[18] Way, W. and Holden, K., 2009. "Teachers' Background and Capacity to Teach Personal Finance: Results of a National Study." Association for Financial Counseling and Planning Education.
(http://www.nefe.org/LinkClick.aspx?fileticket=q9Ahp7m5Cbg%3d&tabid=246)

[19] *Ibid.*

[20] *Ibid,* FINRA National Survey on Financial Capability.

[21] American Council on Education, 2006. "Missed Opportunities Revised: New Information on Students Who Do Not Apply for Financial Aid." http://www.acenet.edu/AM/Template.cfm?Section=Home&TEMPLATE=/CM/ContentDisplay.cfm&CONTENTI D=33967

[22] *Ibid,* Dora, G.T.

[23] Edmiston, Kelly D., Mary C. Gillett-Fisher and Molly McGrath, 2009. "Weighing the Effects of Financial Education in the Workplace." The Federal Reserve Bank of Kansas City, Community Affairs Department Research Working Paper.

[24] Kim, Jinhee, Benoit Sorhaindo and E. Thomas Garman, 2006. "Relationship between Financial Stress and Workplace Absenteeism of Credit Counseling Clients." *Journal of Family and Economic Issues*, Volume 27, Number 3, Pages 458-478

[25] Garman, E.T., Leech, I.E. & Grable, J.E. (1996). The negative impact of employee poor personal financial behaviors on employers. Financial Counseling and Planning, 7, 157-168.

[26] Bailey, Woodiel, Turner, and Young, 1998. "The Relationship of Financial Stress to Overall Stress and Satisfaction, Personal Finances and Worker Productivity." Personal Finance Employee Education Foundation. http://www.personalfinancefoundation.org/research/efd/Personal-Finances-and-Worker-Productivity.html

[27] Thaler, R.H. and Sunstein, C.R., 2008. *Nudge: Improving Decisions About Health, Wealth and Happiness*.

[28] Nelson, Thomas, 2008. "How to Implement an Automatic 401(k) Plan and Increase Employee Contributions." International Foundation of Employee Benefit Plans. http://www.retirementmadesimpler.org/Library/NelsonJulyBC.pdf

[29] Madrian, B. and Shea, D.F., 2001. "The Power of Suggestion: Inertia in 401(k) Participation and Savings Behavior. *The Quarterly Journal of Economics.* Vol. 205 Issue 4. http://www.retirementmadesimpler.org/Library/The%20Power%20of%20Suggestion-%20Inertia%20in%20401(k).pdf

[30] Beshears, J., Choi, J., Laibson, D., Madrian B.C., Weller, B., 2010. "Public Policy and Saving for Retirement: The 'Autosave' Features of the Pension Protection Act of 2006." John J. Siegfried, editor. *Better Living Through Economics.*

[31] *Ibid,* Beshears et al., 2010.

[32] Nelson, Thomas, 2008. "How to Implement an Automatic 401(k) Plan and Increase Employee Contributions." International Foundation of Employee Benefit Plans. http://www.retirementmadesimpler.org/Library/NelsonJulyBC.pdf

[33] VanDerhei, Jack L., 2007. "The Expected Impact of Automatic Escalation of 401(k) Contribution to Retirement Income." Employee Benefit Research Institute. September 2007, Vol. 28, No. 9 12pp. http://www.ebri.org/publications/notes/?fa=notes Disp& contentid=3844

[34] Copeland, Craig, 2011. "401(k) Participants Who Use TDFs Overwhelmingly Stick With Them." Employee Benefit Research Institute. http://www.ebri.org/pdf/PR935.30Aug11.T-DFunds.pdf

[35] Workplace Leaders in Financial Education Award, "Toolkit: Topic Ideas by SHRM" http://www.wlife.org/InYour-Workplace/Toolkit/Topic-Ideas

[36] Bayer, Patrick J., B. Douglas Bernheim and John Karl Scholz, 2009. "The Effects of Education in the Workplace: Evidence from a Survey of Employers." Economic Inquiry, 47(4): 605-624.

[37] Federal Deposit Insurance Corporation, 2009. "What Works in the Workplace: Helping Employers Provide Financial Education to their Staff." http://www.fdic.gov/consumers/consumer/moneysmart/newsletter/sum2009/stories.html

[38] Personal Finance Employee Education Foundation, "Personal Finance Topics." http://www.pfeef.org/resources/best-resources.html

INDEX

C

D

E

F

S

T

U

V

W

Y